AMERICAN
WAR LIBRARY
★ ★ ★ ★

★ The Cold War ★

PRIMARY SOURCES

Titles in the American War Library series include:

AMERICAN
WAR LIBRARY
★★★★

✯ The Cold War ✯

PRIMARY SOURCES

Edited by Stuart A. Kallen

LUCENT
BOOKS®

THOMSON
★
GALE

San Diego • Detroit • New York • San Francisco • Cleveland • New Haven, Conn. • Waterville, Maine • London • Munich

THOMSON
GALE
™

For more information, contact
Lucent Books
27500 Drake Rd.
Farmington Hills, MI 48331-3535
Or you can visit our Internet site at http://www.gale.com

LIBRARY OF CONGRESS CATALOGING-IN-PUBLICATION DATA

Kallen, Stuart A., 1955–
    Primary sources / by Stuart A. Kallen.
        p. cm. — (American war library. Cold War)
Includes bibliographical references and index.
Summary: Presents the original documents used as source material for the American
War Library, Cold War series.
        ISBN 1-59018-243-X (hardback : alk. paper)
    1. Cold War—Sources—Juvenile literature.   2. United States—Foreign relations—
Soviet Union—Sources.   3. Soviet Union—Foreign relations—United States—Sources.
4. Espionage—Juvenile literature—Sources.   I. Title.   II. American war library.
Cold War series.
    D843 .K328 2003
    226.5'06—dc21
                                                                                2002007896

★ Contents ★

A Nation Forged by War

The United States, like many nations, was forged and defined by war. Despite Benjamin Franklin's opinion that "There never was a good war or a bad peace," the United States owes its very existence to the War of Independence, one to which Franklin wholeheartedly subscribed. The country forged by war in 1776 was tempered and made stronger by the Civil War in the 1860s.

The Texas Revolution, the Mexican-American War, and the Spanish-American War expanded the country's borders and gave it overseas possessions. These wars made the United States a world power, but this status came with a price, as the nation became a key but reluctant player in both World War I and World War II.

Each successive war further defined the country's role on the world stage. Following World War II, U.S. foreign policy redefined itself to focus on the role of defender, not only of the freedom of its own citizens, but also of the freedom of people everywhere. During the Cold War that followed World War II until the collapse of the Soviet Union, defending the world meant fighting communism. This goal, manifested in the Korean and Vietnam conflicts, proved elusive, and soured the American public on its achievability. As the United States emerged as the world's sole superpower, American foreign policy has been guided less by national interest and more on protecting international human rights. But as involvement in Somalia and Kosovo prove, this goal has been equally elusive.

As a result, the country's view of itself changed. Bolstered by victories in World Wars I and II, Americans first relished the role of protector. But, as war followed war in a seemingly endless procession, Americans began to doubt their leaders, their motives, and themselves. The Vietnam War especially caused people to question the validity of sending its young people to die in places where they were not particularly wanted and for people who did not seem especially grateful.

While the most obvious changes brought about by America's wars have been geopolitical in nature, many other aspects of society have been touched. War often does not bring about change directly, but acts instead like the catalyst in a chemical reaction, accelerating changes already in progress.

Some of these changes have been societal. The role of women in the United States had been slowly changing, but World War II put thousands into the workforce and into uniform. They might have gone back to being housewives after the war, but equality, once experienced, would not be forgotten.

Likewise, wars have accelerated technological change. The necessity for faster airplanes and a more destructive bomb led to the development of jet planes and nuclear energy. Artificial fibers developed for parachutes in the 1940s were used in the clothing of the 1950s.

Lucent Books' American War Library covers key wars in the development of the nation. Each war is covered in several volumes, to allow for more detail and context, and to provide volumes on often neglected subjects, such as the kamikazes of World War II, or weapons used in the Civil War. As with all Lucent Books, notes, annotated bibliographies, and appendixes such as glossaries give students a launching point for further research. In addition, sidebars and archival photographs enhance the text. Together, each volume in The American War Library will aid students in understanding how America's wars have shaped and changed its politics, economics, and society.

Chapter 1

An Uneasy Peace

When the guns of World War II fell silent in 1945, two allies, the United States and the Union of Soviet Socialist Republics (U.S.S.R.), were left as the most powerful nations on earth. Although the shooting was over, a state of constant, nonviolent hostility known as the Cold War arose between the two superpowers.

The Cold War first began in the late 1940s, after the Soviet Union extended its influence over much of war-torn Eastern Europe. The Soviets imposed repressive government dictatorships upon East Germany, Poland, Czechoslovakia, Hungary, Bulgaria, and other nations; these countries became known as the Eastern bloc. In these countries, government officials controlled nearly every aspect of life. They provided free health care, schooling, housing, clothing, and other amenities. But bureaucrats also dictated where people worked, what goods were available in the stores, what was printed in newspapers,

and even what people were allowed to say to one another.

This control was enforced by millions of secret police agents stationed in nearly every workplace and public place. Citizens who protested or contradicted government policy were sometimes exiled to concentration camps or killed. Some Soviet experts estimate that at least 2 million people were in government prison camps at any given time for political offenses and 10 million were executed during the postwar years.

Conditions were so bad in the Eastern bloc that millions of people tried to leave. But strict government bans on travel—and tight control over borders—prevented a mass exodus, and the only successful emigrants were those who escaped secretly.

A third player was added to the Cold War equation in October 1949, when China fell to the Chinese Communist Party. This Communist revolution placed close to 500 million Chinese people under totalitarian rule. With 220 million Soviets already living under the dictatorial system, more than one-quarter of the world's population was now living under Communist control. This struck terror into the hearts of many Americans who were afraid that these countries might join forces and attempt an armed takeover of Asia, Western Europe, or even the United States.

Between the 1950s and the early 1990s, the United States and the Soviet Union spent trillions of dollars on weapons and armies. This led to a decades-long military standoff in which the two superpowers pointed thousands of nuclear missiles at each other. For the first time in history, two powerful enemies had the ability to destroy the world.

Such an end never came, however. Although the verbal battles between the superpowers often reached a fevered pitch, the Cold War ended without a direct confrontation between the United States and the U.S.S.R. ever taking place. But during those anxious decades when the Cold War was a threat, the conflict dominated nearly every aspect of life and politics in the world.

Churchill's "Iron Curtain" Speech

After Germany was defeated in World War II, the U.S.S.R. imposed a police state on Poland, Bulgaria, Hungary, and other Eastern European countries formerly occupied by the Ger-

mans. On March 6, 1946, less than ten months after Germany's defeat, British wartime prime minister Winston Churchill appeared at Westminster College in Fulton, Missouri, where he received an honorary degree. There, Churchill gave the following speech contending that the Soviet Union threatened a large portion of Europe since they curtailed free speech and elective government in their own country and the nations they controlled—and because they prevented their citizens from finding a better life elsewhere. In the speech Churchill stated that the Soviets had erected an "iron curtain" across Eastern Europe. This term came to be universally accepted as a definition of Soviet power throughout the Cold War.

I am glad to come to Westminster College this afternoon and am complimented that you should give me a degree. . . . It is also an honor, perhaps almost unique, for a private visitor to be introduced to an academic audience by [Harry Truman] the President of the United States. . . . [The] President has traveled a thousand miles to dignify and magnify our meeting here today and give me an opportunity of addressing this kindred nation, as well as my own countrymen across the ocean and perhaps some other countries, too. The President has told you that it is his wish, as I am sure it is yours, that I should have full liberty to give my true and faithful counsel in these anxious and baffling times. . . . I can, therefore, allow my mind, with the experience of a lifetime, to play over the problems which beset us on the

British prime minister Winston Churchill warns the world of the dangers posed by the Soviet police state.

morrow of our absolute victory in arms [during World War II], and try to make sure that what has been gained with so much sacrifice and suffering shall be preserved for the future glory and safety of mankind. . . .

I now come to the . . . danger which threatens . . . ordinary people, namely tyranny. We cannot be blind to the fact that the liberties enjoyed by individual citizens throughout [the United States and] the British Empire are not valid in a considerable number of countries, some of which are very powerful. In these states, control is enforced upon the common people by various kinds of all-embracing police governments, to a degree which is overwhelming and contrary to every principle of democracy. The power of the state is exercised without restraint, either by dictators or by compact oligarchies [small groups of rulers] operating through a privileged party and a political police. It is not our duty at this time, when difficulties are so numerous, to interfere forcibly in the internal affairs of countries whom we have not conquered in war, but we must never cease to proclaim in fearless tones the great principles of freedom and the rights of man, which are the joint inheritance of the English-speaking world and which, through. . . the Bill of Rights, . . . trial by jury and the English common law, find their most famous expression in the Declaration of Independence.

All this means that the people of any country have the right and should have the power by constitutional action, by free, unfettered [unrestricted] elections, with secret ballot, to choose or change the character or form of government under which they dwell, that freedom of speech and thought should reign, that courts of justice independent of the executive, unbiased by any party, should administer laws which have received the broad assent [consent] of large majorities or are consecrated [made sacred] by time and custom. Here are the title deeds of freedom, which should lie in every cottage home. Here is the message of the British and American peoples to mankind. Let us preach what we practice and practice what we preach. . . .

A shadow has fallen upon the scenes so lately lighted by the Allied victory [in Europe]. Nobody knows what Soviet Russia and its Communist international organization intends to do in the immediate future, or what are the limits, if any, to their expansive . . . tendencies. . . .

An Iron Curtain Has Fallen

It is my duty . . . , however, to place before you certain facts about the present position in Europe—I am sure I do not wish to, but it is my duty, I feel, to present them to you.

From Stettin [Poland] in the Baltic [Sea] to Triest [Italy] in the Adriatic [Sea], an iron curtain has descended across the Continent [Europe]. Behind that line lie all the capitals of the ancient states of central and eastern Europe. Warsaw, Berlin, Prague, Vienna, Budapest, Belgrade, Bucharest and Sofia, all these famous cities

and the populations around them lie in the Soviet sphere and all are subject in one form or another, not only to Soviet influence but to a very high and increasing measure of control from Moscow [the Soviet capital]. Athens alone, with its immortal glories, is free to decide its future at an election under British, American and French observation. . . . The Communist parties, which were very small in all these eastern states of Europe, have been raised to pre-eminence and power far beyond their numbers and are seeking everywhere to obtain totalitarian control. Police governments are prevailing in nearly every case, and so far, except in Czechoslovakia, there is no true democracy. . . . Whatever conclusions may be drawn from these facts—and facts they are—this is certainly not the liberated Europe we fought to build up. Nor is it one which contains the essentials of permanent peace. In front of the iron curtain which lies across Europe are other causes for anxiety. In Italy the Communist party is seriously hampered by having to support the Communist trained Marshal Tito's claims to former Italian territory [in Yugoslavia] at the head of the Adriatic. . . . [In] a great number of countries, far from the Russian frontiers and throughout the world, Communist [organizers] are established and work in complete unity and absolute obedience to the directions they receive from the Communist center. Except in the British Commonwealth and in this United States, where Communism is in its infancy,

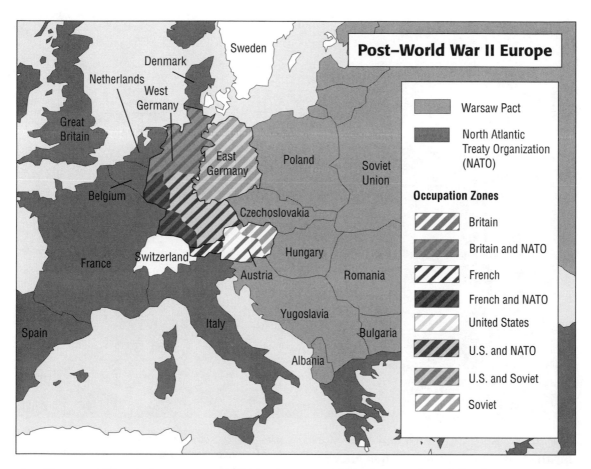

the Communist parties . . . constitute a growing challenge and peril to Christian civilization. . . .

I repulse the idea that a new war is inevitable; still more that it is imminent. It is because I am so sure that our fortunes are in our own hands and that we hold the power to save the future, that I feel the duty to speak out now that I have an occasion to do so. I do not believe that Soviet Russia desires war. What they desire is the fruits of war and the indefinite expansion of their power and doctrines. But what we have to

consider here today while time remains, is the permanent prevention of war and the establishment of conditions of freedom and democracy as rapidly as possible in all countries. Our difficulties and dangers will not be removed by closing our eyes to them. They will not be removed by mere waiting to see what happens; nor will they be relieved by a policy of appeasement [peacemaking]. What is needed is a settlement and the longer this is delayed the more difficult it will be and the greater our dangers will become. From what I have

seen of our Russian friends and allies during the war, I am convinced that there is nothing they admire so much as strength, and there is nothing for which they have less respect than for military weakness. . . .

If the population of the English-speaking commonwealth be added to that of the United States, with all that such co-operation implies in the air, on the sea and in science and industry, there will be no quivering, precarious balance of power to offer its temptation to ambition or adventure. On the contrary, there will be an overwhelming assurance of security. If we adhere faithfully to the charter of the

After the dissolution of the "iron curtain" the border crossing into the Soviet sector is quiet. A checkpoint official sits and reads the paper to pass the time.

United Nations and walk forward in sedate and sober strength, seeking no one's land or treasure, or seeking to lay no arbitrary control on the thoughts of men, if all British moral and material forces and convictions are joined with your own in fraternal association, the highroads of the future will be clear, not only for us but for all, not only for our time but for a century to come.

Winston Churchill, "The Sinews of Peace," address delivered at Westminster College, Fulton, Missouri, March 5, 1946.

Mao Tse-tung Predicts America's Downfall

The Cold War between the United States and the U.S.S.R. became a tense three-way standoff when Communist leader Mao Tse-tung gained control in China in October 1949. Even before that event, in late 1947, Mao wrote of the coming struggle between the Communists, whom he refers to as democratic and the United States, whose policies he deemed imperialist because of the U.S. tendency to extend political and economic authority over other nations. In the following report issued by Mao, the Chinese leader also predicted a catastrophic loss for the United States in the coming battle between the Communists and the Americans.

America's strength is superficial and transient. The crisis [pending communist takeover of China] is like a volcano that menaces American imperialism every day. American imperialism is sitting on this volcano. This situation has driven the American imperialists to draw up a plan for enslaving the world; to run amuck like wild beasts in Europe, Asia, and other parts of the world; to muster the reactionary forces in all countries, the human dregs cast off by their peoples; to form an imperialist, anti-democratic camp against all the democratic forces headed by the Soviet Union; and to prepare for war in the hope that in the future at a distant time, some day, they can start a third world war to defeat the democratic [communist] forces. This is a preposterous plan. The dem-

ocratic [communist] forces of the world must and certainly can defeat this plan. The strength of the world anti-imperialist camp has surpassed that of the imperialist camp. It is we, not the enemy [the United States], who are in the superior position. The anti-imperialist camp headed by the Soviet Union has already been formed. The socialist Soviet Union is free from crisis, in the ascendancy [in control], and cherished by the world's broad masses: its strength has already surpassed that of the imperialist United States, which is seriously menaced by crises, on the decline, and opposed by the world's broad masses. The people's democracies [communists] in Europe are consolidating themselves internally and are uniting with each other. In the European capitalist countries the people's anti-imperialist forces are developing, with those in France and Italy taking the lead. Within the United States, there are people's democratic forces that are getting stronger every day. The peoples of Latin America are not slaves obedient to U.S. imperialism. In the whole of Asia a great national liberation movement has arisen. All the forces of the anti-imperialist camp are uniting and forging ahead. The communist and workers' parties of nine European countries have . . . issued a call to the people of the world to rise against the imperialist plan of enslavement. This call to battle has inspired the oppressed people of the world, charted the course of their struggle, and strengthened their confidence in victory. It has thrown world reaction into panic and confusion. All the anti-imperialist forces in the countries of the East, too, should unite, oppose oppression by imperialism and by their domestic reactionaries, and make the emancipation [freedom] of the more than one billion oppressed people of the East the goal of their struggle.

Mao Tse-tung criticizes American foreign policy as imperialistic.

We must grasp our own destiny in our own hands. We should rid our ranks of all impotent [weak] thinking. All views that overestimate the strength of the enemy and underestimate the strength of the people are wrong. If everyone makes strenuous efforts, we, together with all the democratic [communist] forces of the world, can surely defeat the imperialist plan of enslavement, prevent the outbreak of a third world war, overthrow all reactionary regimes, and win lasting peace for mankind. . . . This is the historic epoch [era] in which world capitalism and imperialism are going down to their doom and world socialism and democracy are marching to victory. The dawn is in sight, we must exert ourselves. . . .

How different is the logic of the imperialists from that of the people! Make trouble, fail, make trouble again, fail again, till their doom; that is the logic of the imperialists and all reactionaries the world over, and they will never go against this logic. This is a Marxist truth. When we say 'imperialism is ferocious', we mean that its nature will never change, that the imperialists will never lay down their butcher knives, that they will never become [enlightened] till their doom. . . .

At present another situation has to be taken into account, namely, that the war maniacs [in the United States] may drop atomic and hydrogen bombs everywhere. They drop them and we drop them too; thus there will be chaos and lives will be lost. The question has to be considered for the worst. The Political Bureau of our

Party has held several sessions to discuss this question. If fighting breaks out now, China has got only hand grenades and not atomic bombs, but the Soviet Union has them. Let us imagine how many people will die if war should break out? Out of the world's population of 2,700 million [2.7 billion], one third—or, putting the figure a bit higher, half—may be lost. It is they and not we who want to fight; when a fight starts, atomic and hydrogen bombs will be dropped. I debated this question with a foreign statesman. He believed that if an atomic war was fought, the whole of mankind might be annihilated. I said that if the worst came to the worst and half of mankind died, the other half would remain while imperialism would be razed to the ground [completely destroyed] and the whole world would become socialist. In a certain number of years, there would be 2,700 million people again and definitely more. We Chinese have not yet completed our [revolution] and we desire peace. However, if imperialism insists on fighting a war, we will have no alternative but to make up our minds and fight it, before going ahead with our [revolution]. . . .

The policies of aggression and war of U.S. imperialism also seriously threaten the Soviet Union, China, and the other socialist countries. Moreover, it [U.S. imperialism] is vigorously seeking to push its policy of 'peaceful evolution' in the socialist countries, in order to bring about the restoration of capitalism there and disintegrate the socialist camp. . . .

The people of the countries in the socialist camp should unite, the people of all the countries of Asia, Africa, and Latin America should unite, the people of all the continents of the world should unite, all peace-loving countries and all countries that are subject to U.S. aggression, control, interference and bullying should unite, and so form the broadest united front to oppose the U.S. imperialist policies of aggression and war and to safeguard world peace.

Riding roughshod everywhere, U.S. imperialism has placed itself in the position of the enemy of the people the world over, and has increasingly isolated itself. The atom bombs and hydrogen bombs in the hands of the U.S. imperialists can never cow [intimidate] people not willing to be enslaved. The raging tide of the people of the world in opposition to the U.S. aggressors is irresistible. The struggle of the people the world over against U.S. imperialism and its running dogs will assuredly win still greater victories.

Mao Tse-tung, excerpt of a report issued December 25, 1947.

The Clash of Civilizations

In 1950, U.S. State Department planner Paul Nitze drafted a policy paper, called NSC-68, that explained the profound differences in ideology between the United States and the Soviet Union. One of the most important documents of the Cold War, NSC-68 called on the United States to spend any amount of money necessary—and use any weapons available—in order to triumph over the worldwide Communist movement. After the ideas in this document won the approval of President Truman, U.S. military spending tripled. Used as the blueprint for U.S.

Paul Nitze wrote policy that defines the differences in ideology between the Soviets and the Americans.

military policy for years, the concepts described by NSC-68 were frightening. The policy paper predicted an inevitable nuclear battle between Communist countries and Western democracies—a war that could leave the entire planet in ruins. In the excerpt from NSC-68 below, Nitze describes the political forces that created this situation between the two superpowers.

Within the past thirty-five years the world has experienced two global wars of tremendous violence. It has witnessed two revolutions—the Russian and the Chinese—of extreme scope and intensity. It has also seen the collapse of five empires—the Ottoman, the Austro-Hungarian, German, Italian and Japanese—and the drastic decline of two major imperial systems, the British and the French. During the span of one generation, the international distribution of power has been fundamentally altered. For several centuries it had proved impossible for any one nation to gain such preponderant strength that a coalition of other nations could not in time face it with greater strength. The international scene was marked by recurring periods of violence and war, but a system of sovereign and independent states was maintained, over which no state was able to achieve hegemony [domination].

Two complex sets of factors have now basically altered this historical distribution of power. First, the defeat of Germany and Japan and the decline of the British and French Empires have interacted with the development of the United States and the

Soviet Union in such a way that power has increasingly gravitated to these two centers. Second, the Soviet Union, unlike previous aspirants to hegemony, is animated by a new fanatic faith [communism], antithetical [hostile] to our own, and seeks to impose its absolute authority over the rest of the world. Conflict has, therefore, become endemic [widespread] and is waged, on the part of the Soviet Union, by violent or non-violent methods in accordance with the dictates of expediency. With the development of increasingly terrifying weapons of mass destruction, every individual faces the ever-present possibility of annihilation should the conflict enter the phase of total war.

On the one hand, the people of the world yearn for relief from the anxiety arising from the risk of atomic war. On the other hand, any substantial further extension of the area under the domination of the Kremlin [Soviet government] would raise the possibility that no coalition adequate to confront the Kremlin with greater strength could be assembled. It is in this context that this Republic [the United States] and its citizens in the ascendancy [superiority] of their strength stand in their deepest peril.

The issues that face us are momentous, involving the fulfillment or destruction not only of this Republic but of civilization itself. They are issues which will not await our deliberations. With conscience and resolution this Government and the people it represents must now [make] new and fateful decisions.

Fundamental Purpose of the United States

The fundamental purpose of the United States is laid down in the Preamble to the Constitution: ". . . to form a more perfect Union, establish Justice, insure domestic Tranquility, provide for the common defence, promote the general Welfare, and secure the Blessings of Liberty to ourselves and our Posterity." In essence, the fundamental purpose is to assure the integrity and vitality of our free society, which is founded upon the dignity and worth of the individual.

Three realities emerge as a consequence of this purpose: Our determination to maintain the essential elements of individual freedom, as set forth in the Constitution and Bill of Rights; our determination to create conditions under which our free and democratic system can live and prosper; and our determination to fight if necessary to defend our way of life, for which as in the Declaration of Independence, "with a firm reliance on the protection of Divine Providence, we mutually pledge to each other our lives, our Fortunes and our sacred Honor."

Fundamental Plan of the Kremlin

The fundamental design of those who control the Soviet Union and the international communist movement is to retain and solidify their absolute power, first in the Soviet Union and second in the areas now under their control. In the minds of the Soviet leaders, however, achievement of this design requires the dynamic extension of their authority and the ultimate elimination of any effective opposition to their authority.

The design, therefore, calls for the complete subversion or forcible destruction of the machinery of government and structure of society in the countries of the non-Soviet world and their replacement by an apparatus and structure subservient to and controlled from the Kremlin. To that end Soviet efforts are now directed toward the domination of the Eurasian land mass. The United States, as the principal center of power in the non-Soviet world and the bulwark [protective barrier] of opposition to Soviet expansion, is the principal enemy whose integrity and vitality must be subverted or destroyed by one means or another if the Kremlin is to achieve its fundamental design.

The Kremlin regards the United States as the only major threat to the achievement of its fundamental design. There is a basic conflict between the idea of freedom under a government of laws, and the idea of slavery under . . . the Kremlin, which has come to a crisis with the polarization [division] of power . . . and the exclusive possession of atomic weapons by the two protagonists. The idea of freedom, moreover, is peculiarly and intolerably subversive of the idea of slavery. But the converse is not true. The implacable [unchangeable] purpose of the slave state to eliminate the challenge of freedom has placed the two great powers at opposite poles. It is this fact which gives the present polarization of power the quality of crisis.

Paul Nitze, excerpt of NSC-68, a report to the president pursuant to the president's directive of January 31, 1950.

A Brief Thaw in the Cold War

In 1959, there was a slight thaw in the Cold War. During this period, the United States and the Soviet Union agreed to hold a cultural exchange in order to learn more about one another's cultures and economies. The United States staged a national exhibition in Moscow, while the Soviets reciprocated in New York City. More than 1 million Americans viewed the Soviet show, which displayed the scientific and technological accomplishments of the socialist state. Almost 3 million Soviets attended the American exhibition, which displayed consumer goods such as washing machines and automobiles, along with Hollywood movies and other cultural icons. Under the repressive Communist regime, however, Soviet visitors were discouraged from expressing too much enthusiasm for the American way of life. Those who did praise capitalism were harassed by the secret police patrolling through the crowd. The following excerpt from a U.S. State Department report analyzes the exchange.

The first exchange of exhibitions between the United States and the Soviet Union ended on September 6 with the closing of the American fair in Sokolniki Park in Moscow. The Soviet exhibition had closed in New York on August 10. An estimated 2.5 to 3 million Soviet citizens visited the

US exhibition during its 43-day run, while the Soviet exhibition was seen by well over a million Americans during its somewhat shorter run. Despite certain negative aspects of the exchange, both sides viewed the outcome as successful.

The Soviet Union appeared to be well pleased by the favorable reaction to its exhibition, which was seen at the New York Coliseum from July 25 to August 10. The Soviet press generally approved of the reception accorded the exhibit, though it did take issue with those US commentators who pointed out that many of the goods on display were not representative of what was generally available in the USSR. . . .

The focal point of the exhibition was the central area dominated by the heroic statue of a steel worker and a collection of sputniks [unmanned Soviet satellites]. Simplicity and terseness contributed to the effectiveness of the relatively few propaganda slogans on view. These were devoted for the most part to three central themes: (1) peace and good relations with foreign countries; (2) Soviet economic progress; and (3) the social benefits of the Soviet system.

Soviet premier Nikita Khrushchev (center, left) and U.S. vice president Richard Nixon discuss national issues as they view an American kitchen exhibit in Moscow.

The inclusion of consumers' goods in the exhibit struck a light note and was well received by the US press. Soviet correspondents were quick to report that Russian fashion models were getting front-page pictures in American newspapers while sultry Italian movie stars were being relegated to small notices on the inside pages. Despite their good press, the consumers' goods displays had perhaps the least impact upon American visitors, who for the most part were well aware that the merchandise shown was not what was being offered to the Soviet consumer. . . .

The Soviet exhibition differed most strikingly from its American counterpart in Moscow in the degree to which it was accessible to the public. Tickets could be bought at the Coliseum box office (adults $1, children 50 cents) by anyone. Moreover, those Americans who did not visit the exhibit had ample opportunity to become acquainted with it through extensive and generally favorable newspaper reports. Because of its novelty, the relatively small exhibit, with only about 15,000 square yards of floor space, commanded an unprecedented amount of space in the American press.

The US Exhibition in Moscow

The American fair in Moscow enjoyed considerable success in spite of strenuous and concerted Soviet efforts to discredit it. While the attitude of the Soviet Government remained officially correct, Soviet propagandists conducted a well-planned campaign to belittle the exhibition in the eyes of the Russian people. The campaign, which began some weeks before the opening of the fair, expanded significantly after July 25, the opening date, and the volume of propaganda continued thereafter at a high level. . . .

The Soviet propaganda effort proceeded along two main lines: (1) disparagement of the fair as a whole and of certain exhibits in particular, and (2) an increased emphasis in the Soviet press on the more negative side of American life, i.e., unemployment, bad housing, slums, etc. Attempts to discredit the fair itself began with an attack on the model house, which in a press conference was described by Ambassador Menshikov as beyond the means of the average American and by the Soviet press as no more like the home of a typical American worker than the Taj Mahal is like the home of a worker in Bombay [India]. The Soviet press also seized eagerly upon criticisms in the United States leveled against the art exhibit and the racial integration portrayed in the fashion show.

With the opening of the fair, Soviet propaganda moved into high gear. Continuing to play upon the theme that the goods on display were obtainable only by the rich, the press attacked the fair for showing only the favorable side of American life. . . . Criticism of a harsher sort was daily expressed by agitators planted on the grounds outside the fair, in the streets, and reportedly in the factories. Agitators in large numbers

Khrushchev (left), Nixon (right), and other dignitaries share a friendly moment at Sokloniki Park.

also entered the fair grounds, where they stationed themselves near the various exhibits in order to embarrass the guides and other Americans present with "loaded" questions. . . .

Propaganda was supplemented by various kinds of obstructionism and harassment. Soviet authorities requested the removal of a considerable number of books from the display, including such innocuous [harmless] items as the World Almanac, on the grounds that they contained "anti-Soviet propaganda.". . .

Ticket distribution, which was entirely under Soviet control, was handled through local [Communist] Party organizations in such a way as to favor individuals of political reliability. Ticket booths in Moscow were deliberately uncooperative in providing information on where tickets could be obtained, and tickets went on public sale only during the second week of the fair. "Public sale," as it turned out, meant sale to those whose names appeared on an approved list, and conversations with Soviet citizens revealed that not everyone was eligible to receive this favor. . . .

The variety of measures inaugurated [put in place] by Soviet authorities to counteract the effects of the American fair and the degree of control instituted over Soviet visitors to the fair shows clearly the limits which the Soviet Government sets on "free exchanges" with the West. Even on the fair grounds the Soviet citizen was not free from surveillance and control. Instances of police intimidation of Soviet citizens were directly observed on a number of occasions, and by the end of the first week four arrests had been reported of individuals seen to have been speaking long and freely on political subjects with the guides. Known KGB [secret police] agents were in constant attendance. . . .

Popular Soviet reaction to the exhibition was one of intense interest and general approval. Soviet visitors displayed enormous curiosity not only about the exhibits but about all facets of American life, and the American Russian-speaking guides, who were called upon for information on every conceivable subject, themselves became objects of interest and approval. The Negro guides made a distinct impression upon the visitors, since their appearance and obvious education conflicted strongly with the stereotype of the American Negro created by Soviet propaganda.

Disappointment at the absence of heavy machinery and other tangible examples of American technical achievements appeared to be to some extent genuine. Accustomed to such exhibits in their own country, Soviet citizens apparently hoped for a similar display of American technology. Also disappointing to Soviet visitors was the apparent lack of focus of the fair as a whole. While the aim of showing the wide variety of elements that go to make up American life may have been achieved, the effect upon the Soviet citizen, who is used to having things spelled out, may have been somewhat perplexing. A further criticism voiced by some of the visitors was the relative lack of emphasis upon religious life in the United States. . . .

American automobiles and color television appeared to be two of the most popular exhibits at the fair. . . . Visitors invariably asked detailed questions about costs, amount of working time required to earn the purchase price, waiting period required, etc. The model house, the fashion show, the IBM question-answering machine and Pepsi-Cola were all extremely popular exhibits. The book corner proved to be a highly frequented area, the most popular works being books on art, architecture, and the sciences. Evidence of the interest shown by Soviet citizens in Western books was the rapid disappearance of books (some 600 the first day). Losses from the bookmobile were so high that the exhibit had to be closed until a new shipment of books could be flown in.

U.S. Department of State, excerpt of Foreign Relations Series, 1958–1960, no. 10, 1.

U.S. Response to Czech Crackdown

In early 1968, the leaders of Czechoslovakia en-acted democratic reforms, rejected censorship, and began to resist the Soviet rule that had been im-posed on their country after World War II. In August, however, tanks from several Soviet-dominated countries (the Soviet Union, East Ger-many, Hungary, and others) rolled into the Czechoslovakian capital of Prague to crush the re-bellion. The conflict was violent, and it surprised U.S. leaders because it came at a time when the U.S.S.R. and the West had achieved détente, a pe-riod during which tensions began to ease. In the following excerpt, a U.S. National Security Coun-cil (NSC) document explains the steps it believed the United States should take in order to show dis-satisfaction with the Czech crackdown.

The August 20–21 occupation of Czecho-slovakia . . . provided a cold [shower] for the future of detente, or the progressive rapprochement [reconciliation] of East and West. In the late Sixties, the achieve-ment of detente had become an important objective in the policies of most Western European nations as well as the United States. It had become a key element in the work program of the North Atlantic Treaty Organization [NATO]. But its assumed basis was seriously undermined by the Czechoslovak crisis.

Most Western nations have reacted with strong expressions of disgust at, and disap-proval of, the . . . occupation of independent Czechoslovakia. There was almost universal support for the United Nations considera-tion of this problem. . . .

To give further meaning to their disap-proval, most Western nations undertook to limit contacts with the Soviets and the occu-pying powers . . . , and cancelled plans or proposed visits in the political and cultural fields. As the repression of Czechoslovakia continues, . . . the deterioration of East-West contacts may well continue.

These relatively limited actions do not necessarily preclude the possibility of re-turn in due course to the pursuit of de-tente. The present disposition of many European nations is to avoid actions which might impair the eventual resumption of closer relations with the Soviet Union and the countries of Eastern Europe. . . .

US actions have so far generally paral-leled those of its Western European allies. For the time being we are seeking a bal-anced approach that will satisfy the im-mediate objective of expressing censure [dissatisfaction] of Soviet action without destroying overnight our longer-range goals.

In the cultural field we propose the fol-lowing criteria:

a. Cancel or postpone highly visible ex-changes susceptible to being interpreted as evidence of goodwill or friendship toward

Soviet troops and tanks invade the streets of Prague, Czechoslovakia.

the invading powers. (For example, the trip of the Minnesota Band to Russia.)

b. We do not propose disrupting low-visibility exchanges already in progress. (For example, graduate students, individual scientists and researchers already on study tours.) But we should discourage new initiatives.

c. We should avoid across-the-board restrictive measures, such as indiscriminate restrictions on travel that could be construed as a return to the cold war.

d. We should maintain exchange activities with Czechoslovakia to the extent

possible, and with the still-independent state of Romania. In Czechoslovakia, for instance, we should participate in the Trade Fair at Brno if the Czechoslovak Government decides to hold it. . . .

In the area of peace and security, important decisions will need to be taken. For example, should we agree to open missile talks at any definite early date. Similar decisions involve US participation in the solar eclipse experimentation in the

USSR, US-USSR discussions on peaceful nuclear devices, etc.

In the economic area we should discourage the development of new commercial activities with the aggressor states, and we are considering a curtailment of export licenses.

National Security Council, "The United States, Europe, and the Czechoslovakia Crisis," Foreign Relations Series, 1964–1968, no. 17.

Reagan Calls Soviet Union an "Evil Empire"

On March 8, 1983, President Ronald Reagan addressed the Annual Convention of the National Association of Evangelicals in Orlando, Florida. In a strongly worded speech, excerpted below, the president called the Soviet Union an "evil empire" and refused calls for a nuclear freeze. The president's supporters commended him for his tough talk, but his critics feared that such opinions could seriously harm U.S.–Soviet relations.

During my first press conference as president, in answer to a direct question, I point out that, as good Marxist-Leninists, the Soviet leaders have openly and publicly declared that the only morality they recognize is that which will further their cause, which is world revolution. I think I should point out I was only quoting [Soviet founder Vladimir] Lenin, their guiding spirit, who said in 1920 that they repudiate all morality that proceeds from supernatural ideas—that's their name for religion. . . . Morality is entirely subordinate to the interests of class war. And every-

thing is moral that is necessary for the annihilation [destruction] of the old, exploiting social order and for uniting the proletariat [working peoples].

Well, I think the refusal of many influential people to accept this elementary fact of Soviet doctrine illustrates a historical reluctance to see totalitarian powers for what they are. We saw this phenomenon in the 1930s [in Adolf Hitler's Nazi Germany]. We see it too often today.

This doesn't mean we should isolate ourselves and refuse to seek an understanding with them [the Soviets]. I intend to do everything I can to persuade them of our peaceful intent, to remind them that it was the West that refused to use its nuclear monopoly in the forties and fifties for territorial gain and which now proposes a 50-percent cut in strategic ballistic missiles and the elimination of an entire class of land-based, intermediate-range nuclear missiles.

At the same time, however, they must be made to understand we will never compromise our principles and standards. We will never give away our freedom. We will never abandon our belief in God. And we will never stop searching for a genuine peace. But we can assure none of these things America stands for through the so-called nuclear freeze solutions proposed by some.

The truth is that a freeze now would be a very dangerous fraud, for that is merely the illusion of peace. The reality is that we must find peace through strength.

President Ronald Reagan tells the world he will not implement a nuclear freeze as long as there are evil societies like the Soviet Union.

I would agree to freeze if only we could freeze the Soviets' global desires. A freeze at current levels of weapons would remove any incentive for the Soviets to negotiate seriously in Geneva [Switzerland] and virtually end our chances to achieve the major arms reductions which we have proposed. Instead, they would achieve their objectives through the freeze.

A freeze would reward the Soviet Union for its enormous and unparalleled military buildup. It would prevent the essential and long overdue modernization of United States and allied defenses and would leave our aging forces increasingly vulnerable. And an honest freeze would require extensive prior negotiations on the systems and numbers to be limited and on the measures to ensure effective verification and compliance. And the kind of a freeze that has been suggested would be virtually impossible to verify. Such a major effort would divert us completely from our current negotiations on achieving substantial reductions. . . .

Yes, let us pray for the salvation of all of those who live in that totalitarian darkness—pray they will discover the joy of knowing God. But until they do, let us be aware that while they preach the supremacy of the state, declare its omnipotence [complete power] over individual man, and predict its eventual domination of all peoples on the earth, they are the focus of evil in the modern world. . . . So, in your discussions of the nuclear freeze proposals, I urge you to beware the temptation of pride—the temptation of blithely declaring yourselves above it all and label both sides equally at fault, to ignore the facts of history and the aggressive impulses of an evil empire, to simply call the arms race a giant misunderstanding and thereby remove yourself from the struggle between right and wrong and good and evil.

Ronald Reagan, speech before the National Association of Evangelicals, Orlando, Florida, March 8, 1983., http://Reagan.web teamone.com.

★ Chapter 2 ★

The Nuclear Arms Race

During World War II, scientists in the United States worked with the military to develop the first generation of nuclear weapons, bombs that created massive explosions by splitting atoms of highly toxic radioactive material. The first atomic bombs were constructed by the United States in 1945 and were dropped on the Japanese cities of Hiroshima and Nagasaki, ending World War II on the Asian front. Those two small nuclear bombs wounded half a million people and killed more than 1 million, many of whom experienced slow deaths from radiation poisoning. By the 1950s, the United States and the Soviet Union had also developed hydrogen bombs, weapons one hundred times more powerful than those dropped on Japan. The two countries placed these bombs on missiles that were capable of reaching any city in the world within thirty minutes.

As the years passed, each of the superpowers spent billions of dollars to develop bigger bombs and faster, more accurate missiles. This competition was called the nuclear arms race, and it caused a great deal of anxiety among the American public. In response, politicians reassured nervous civilians that an actual nuclear conflict was unlikely. Neither superpower wanted to be the first to launch nuclear missiles because each knew the other would respond immediately, assuring destruction of both nations. This policy, known as "mutually assured destruction" or MAD, has been credited with preventing the superpowers from ever directly going to war.

Despite the concept of MAD, the superpowers did teeter on the brink of nuclear war in 1962 during an event known as the Cuban missile crisis. On October 14, U.S. intelligence services discovered that the Soviet Union was secretly building offensive nuclear missile sites in Cuba, a Communist nation ninety miles off the coast of southern Florida. This new development presented the United States with a dangerous situation; Soviet nuclear weapons in Cuba could reach Los Angeles, New York City, Washington, D.C., and most other American cities within a matter of minutes. When this was reported in newspapers, tens of thousands of Americans began building bomb shelters in their backyards, hoping to create a way to save their families from potential nuclear explosions and radioactive fallout.

The country never experienced the dreaded nuclear attack, however. After two tense weeks, President John Kennedy diffused the conflict and negotiated a settlement with the U.S.S.R. that prevented the Soviets from placing the weapons in Cuba. Although catastrophe was averted, relations between the United States and the Soviet Union remained bitter for the rest of the decade.

In the early 1970s, advanced computer and radar technology allowed a new generation of even deadlier missiles to be built. This concerned many Americans, who demanded that politicians do something to slow the arms race. As a result, the superpowers discussed arms control for the first time. In 1972, negotiators for the United States and the Soviet Union held the historic Strategic Arms Limitation Talks (SALT), which limited some types of nuclear weapons.

By the 1980s, however, a renewed arms race began as the United States deployed the MX Peacekeeper missile. This weapon carried ten nuclear warheads, each capable of being directed at a specific target. In 1983 the Soviets began preparing similar weapons. This prompted U.S. president Ronald Reagan to call for the development of a defensive "space shield" known as the Strategic Defense Initiative (SDI) or, informally, Star Wars. The theory behind this weapons system (which has yet to be proven) is that space-based lasers could be built to sense incoming missiles and shoot them down before they fell on the United States.

Star Wars and the development of extremely deadly nuclear weapons touched off protests in the United States and Europe. Called the "no-nukes" movement, this involved hundreds of thousands of people who took to the streets to protest the threat that nuclear weapons posed to life on earth.

Although nuclear bombs were never used after World War II, at least a dozen nations throughout the world hold thousands of such weapons in their arsenals today, long after the Cold War's end. But talks continue between the former Soviet Union and the United States to secure the weapons and make the world a safer place, as the two former enemies are now allies with common goals.

Face-off over Cuban Nukes

On October 22, 1962, the Cuban missile crisis pushed the two superpowers toward all-out nuclear war. In the following excerpt from a televised address, President John Kennedy warns

LAUNCH POSITION

MISSILE-READY TENTS

MISSILE ERECTORS

a shocked and fearful America about the impending danger.

This government, as promised, has maintained the closest surveillance of the Soviet military buildup on the island of Cuba. Within the past week, unmistakable evidence has established the fact that a series of offensive missile sites is now in preparation on that imprisoned island. The purpose of these bases can be none other than

This photo taken by a U.S. spy plane clearly shows Soviet missile sites under construction in Cuba.

to provide a nuclear strike capability against the Western Hemisphere. . . .

The characteristics of these new missile sites indicate two distinct types of installations. Several of them include medium-range ballistic missiles, capable of carrying a nuclear warhead for a distance of more than a thousand nautical miles. Each of these missiles, in short, is capable of striking Washington, D.C., the Panama Canal, Cape Canaveral, Mexico City, or any other city in the southeastern part of the United States, in Central America, or in the Caribbean area.

Additional sites not yet completed appear to be designed for intermediate-range ballistic missiles—capable of traveling more than twice as far—and thus capable of striking most of the major cities in the Western Hemisphere, ranging as far north as Hudson Bay, Canada, and as far south as Lima, Peru. In addition, jet bombers, capable of carrying nuclear weapons, are now being uncrated and assembled in Cuba, while the necessary air bases are being prepared.

This urgent transformation of Cuba into an important strategic base—by the presence of these large, long-range, and clearly offensive weapons of sudden mass destruction—constitutes an explicit threat to the peace and security of all the Americas. . . . This action also contradicts the repeated assurances of Soviet spokesmen, both publicly and privately delivered, that the arms buildup in Cuba would retain its original defensive character, and that the Soviet Union had no need or desire to station strategic missiles on the territory of any other nation. . . .

"A Clear and Present Danger"

Neither the United States of America nor the world community of nations can tolerate deliberate deception and offensive threats on the part of any nation, large or small. We no longer live in a world where only the actual firing of weapons represents a sufficient challenge to a nation's security to constitute maximum peril. Nuclear weapons are so destructive, and ballistic missiles are so swift, that any substantially increased possibility of their use or any sudden change in their deployment may well be regarded as a definite threat to peace.

For many years, both the Soviet Union and the United States, recognizing this fact, have deployed strategic nuclear weapons with great care, never upsetting the precarious status quo which insured that these weapons would not be used in the absence of some vital challenge. Our own strategic missiles have never been transferred to the territory of any other nation under a cloak of secrecy and deception; and our history—unlike that of the Soviets since the end of World War II—demonstrates that we have no desire to dominate or conquer any other nation or impose our system upon its people. Nevertheless, American citizens have become adjusted to living daily on the bull's-eye of Soviet missiles located inside the U.S.S.R. or in submarines.

In that sense, missiles in Cuba add to an already clear and present danger. . . .

But this secret, swift, and extraordinary buildup of Communist missiles—in an area well known to have a special and historical relationship to the United States and the nations of the Western Hemisphere, in violation of Soviet assurances, and in defiance of American and hemispheric policy—this sudden, clandestine [secret] decision to station strategic weapons for the first time outside of Soviet soil—is a deliberately provocative and unjustified change in the status quo which cannot be accepted by this country, if our courage and our commitments are ever to be trusted again by either friend or foe. . . .

Our unswerving objective, therefore, must be to prevent the use of these missiles against this or any other country, and to secure their withdrawal or elimination from the Western Hemisphere. . . .

Acting, therefore, in the defense of our own security and of the entire Western Hemisphere, and under the authority entrusted to me by the Constitution as endorsed by the resolution of the Congress, I have directed that the following initial steps be taken immediately:

First: To halt this offensive buildup, a strict quarantine [blockade] on all offensive military equipment under shipment to Cuba is being initiated. All ships of any kind bound for Cuba from whatever nation or port will, if found to contain cargoes of offensive weapons, be turned back. . . .

Second: I have directed the continued and increased close surveillance of Cuba and its military buildup. . . . Should these offensive military preparations continue, thus increasing the threat to the hemisphere, further action will be justified. I have directed the Armed Forces to prepare for any eventualities; and I trust that in the interest of both the Cuban people and the

Soviet technicians at the sites, the hazards to all concerned of continuing this threat will be recognized.

Third: It shall be the policy of this nation to regard any nuclear missile launched from Cuba against any nation in the Western Hemisphere as an attack by the Soviet Union on the United States, requiring a full retaliatory response upon the Soviet Union. . . .

President John F. Kennedy informs the nation about missile sites in Cuba that threaten the security of the United States.

"The Cost of Freedom Is High"

I call upon [Soviet leader] Chairman [Nikita] Khrushchev to halt and eliminate this clandestine, reckless, and provocative threat to world peace and to stable relations between our two nations. I call upon him further to abandon this course of world domination, and to join in an historic effort to end the perilous arms race and to transform the history of man. He has an opportunity now to move the world back from the abyss of destruction—by returning to his government's own words that it had no need to station missiles outside its own territory, and withdrawing these weapons from Cuba—by refraining from any action which will widen or deepen the present crisis—and then by participating in a search for peaceful and permanent solutions.

This nation is prepared to present its case against the Soviet threat to peace, and our own proposals for a peaceful world, at any time and in any forum. . . . We have in the past made strenuous efforts to limit the spread of nuclear weapons. We have proposed the elimination of all arms and military bases in a fair and effective disarmament treaty. We are prepared to discuss new proposals for the removal of tensions on both sides—including the possibilities of a genuinely independent Cuba, free to determine its own destiny. We have no wish to war with the Soviet Union—for we are a peaceful people who desire to live in peace with all other peoples.

My fellow citizens: let no one doubt that this is a difficult and dangerous effort on which we have set out. No one can foresee precisely what course it will take or what costs or casualties will be incurred. Many months of sacrifice and self-discipline lie ahead—months in which both our patience and our will will be tested—months in which many threats and denunciations will keep us aware of our dangers. But the greatest danger of all would be to do nothing.

The path we have chosen for the present is full of hazards, as all paths are—but it is the one most consistent with our character and courage as a nation and our commitments around the world. The cost of freedom is always high—but Americans have always paid it. And one path we shall never choose, and that is the path of surrender or submission.

Our goal is not the victory of might, but the vindication of right—not peace at the expense of freedom, but both peace and freedom, here in this hemisphere, and, we hope, around the world. God willing, that goal will be achieved.

John F. Kennedy, address to the nation on the Cuban missile crisis, televised October 22, 1962.

Reagan Calls for a Strategic Defense Missile System

On March 23, 1983, President Ronald Reagan gave a televised speech in which he announced his intention to order the construction of a strategic defense system under the SDI plan. The

President Ronald Reagan announces to the nation his plan for developing defensive, space-based lasers.

SDI would use space-based lasers to shoot down any incoming missiles launched by the Soviet Union. Critics dubbed the multibillion-dollar weapons system "Star Wars," after the popular science fiction movie. Many argued that the system would never work and would violate the 1972 U.S.-Soviet Antiballistic Missile, or ABM, Treaty, which limited defensive systems. Reagan, however, maintained his support for the SDI. In the following excerpt from that speech, he explains why.

My fellow Americans, thank you for sharing your time with me tonight.

The subject I want to discuss with you, peace and national security, is both timely and important. Timely, because I've reached a decision which offers a new hope for our children in the 21st century, a decision I'll tell you about in a few minutes. And important because there's a very big decision that you must make for yourselves. This subject involves the most basic duty that any President and any people share, the duty to protect and strengthen the peace. . . .

The defense policy of the United States is based on a simple premise: The United States does not start fights. We will never be an aggressor. We maintain our strength in order to deter and defend against aggression—to preserve freedom and peace.

Since the dawn of the atomic age, we've sought to reduce the risk of war by maintaining a strong deterrent and by seeking genuine arms control. "Deterrence" means simply this: making sure any adversary who thinks about attacking the United States, or our allies, or our vital interests, concludes that the risks to him outweigh any potential gains. Once he understands that, he won't attack. We maintain the peace through our strength; weakness only invites aggression.

This strategy of deterrence has not changed. It still works. But what it takes to maintain deterrence has changed. It took one kind of military force to deter an attack when we had far more nuclear weapons than any other power; it takes another kind now that the Soviets, for example, have enough accurate and powerful nuclear weapons to destroy virtually all of our missiles on the ground. Now, this is not to say that the Soviet Union is planning to make war on us. Nor do I believe a war is inevitable—quite the contrary. But what must be recognized is that our security is based on being prepared to meet all threats. . . .

For 20 years the Soviet Union has been accumulating enormous military might. They didn't stop when their forces exceeded all requirements of a legitimate defensive capability. And they haven't stopped now. During the past decade and a half, the Soviets have built up a massive arsenal of new strategic nuclear weapons—weapons that can strike directly at the United States.

As an example, the United States introduced its last new intercontinental ballistic missile [ICBM], the Minute Man III, in 1969, and we're now dismantling our even older Titan missiles. But what has the Soviet Union done in these intervening years? Well, since 1969 the Soviet Union has built five new classes of ICBM's, and upgraded these eight times. As a result, their missiles are much more powerful and accurate than they were several years ago, and they continue to develop more, while ours are increasingly obsolete. . . .

But the Soviets are still adding an average of 3 new warheads a week, and now have 1,300. These warheads can reach their targets in a matter of a few minutes. We still have none. So far, it seems that the Soviet definition of parity [equality] is a box score of 1,300 to nothing, in their favor.

There was a time when we were able to offset superior Soviet numbers with higher quality, but today they are building weapons as sophisticated and modern as our own. . . .

Some people may still ask: Would the Soviets ever use their formidable military power? Well, again, can we afford to believe they won't? There is [the Soviet war in] Afghanistan. And in Poland, the Soviets denied the will of the people and in so doing demonstrated to the world how their military power could also be used to intimidate.

The final fact is that the Soviet Union is acquiring what can only be considered an offensive military force. They have continued to build far more intercontinental ballistic missiles than they could possibly need simply to deter an attack. Their conventional forces are trained and equipped not so much to defend against an attack as they are to permit sudden, surprise offensives of their own. . . .

Now, thus far tonight I've shared with you my thoughts on the problems of national security we must face together. My predecessors in the Oval Office [previous presidents] have appeared before you on other occasions to describe the threat posed by Soviet power and have proposed steps to address that threat. But since the advent [beginning] of nuclear weapons, those steps have been increasingly directed toward deterrence of aggression through the promise of retaliation.

This approach to stability through offensive threat has worked. We and our allies have succeeded in preventing nuclear war for more than three decades. In recent months, however, my advisers, including in particular the Joint Chiefs of Staff, have underscored the necessity to break out of a future that relies solely on offensive retaliation for our security. . . .

Let me share with you a vision of the future which offers hope. It is that we embark

The Soviets show a parade of missiles to exhibit their dominant military strength.

on a program to counter the awesome Soviet missile threat with measures that are defensive. Let us turn to the very strengths in technology that spawned our great industrial base and that have given us the quality of life we enjoy today.

What if free people could live secure in the knowledge that their security did not rest upon the threat of instant U.S. retaliation to deter a Soviet attack, that we could intercept and destroy strategic ballistic missiles before they reached our own soil or that of our allies?

I know this is a formidable, technical task, one that may not be accomplished before the end of this century. Yet, current technology has attained a level of sophistication where it's reasonable for us to begin this effort. It will take years, probably decades of effort on many fronts. There will be failures and setbacks, just as there will be successes and breakthroughs. And as we proceed, we must remain constant in preserving the nuclear deterrent and maintaining a solid capability for flexible response. But isn't it worth every investment necessary to free the world from the threat of nuclear war? We know it is. . . .

I clearly recognize that defensive systems have limitations and raise certain problems and ambiguities. If paired with offensive systems, they can be viewed as fostering an aggressive policy, and no one wants that. But with these considerations firmly in mind, I call upon the scientific community in our country, those who gave us nuclear weapons, to turn their great talents now to the cause of mankind and world peace, to give us the means of rendering these nuclear weapons impotent and obsolete.

Tonight, consistent with our obligations of the ABM treaty and recognizing the need for closer consultation with our allies, I'm taking an important first step. I am directing a comprehensive and intensive effort to define a long-term research and development program to begin to achieve our ultimate goal of eliminating the threat posed by strategic nuclear missiles. This could pave the way for arms control measures to eliminate the weapons themselves. We seek neither military superiority nor political advantage. Our only purpose—one all people share—is to search for ways to reduce the danger of nuclear war.

My fellow Americans, tonight we're launching an effort which holds the promise of changing the course of human history. There will be risks, and results take time. But I believe we can do it. As we cross this threshold, I ask for your prayers and your support.

Ronald Reagan, address to the nation announcing SDI, televised March 23, 1983.

Soviets Criticize Reagan's Star Wars

On March 23, 1988, five years after President Ronald Reagan alarmed the Soviet Union by launching the SDI, Soviet author Dmitri Klimov wrote about the initiative in the Soviet

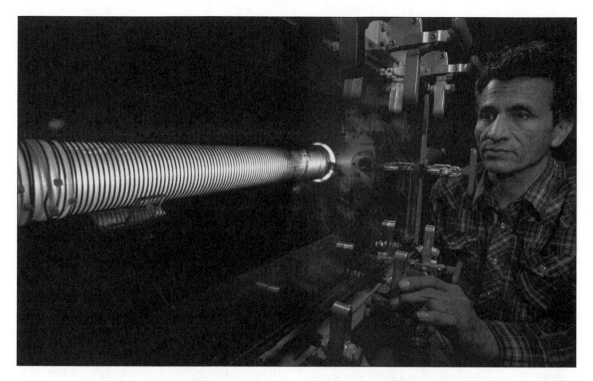

A researcher tests equipment being developed for space-based lasers.

military newspaper Krasnaya Zvezda (Red Star). *According to Klimov, the SDI touched off a dangerous competition between the two superpowers in regard to research, development, and testing of strategic weapons systems. In the following excerpt, Klimov criticizes the United States for working on the development of the SDI, arguing that the program increased the chances of all-out nuclear war.*

It is five years since the day U.S. President Ronald Reagan proclaimed the program for the establishment of a large-scale ABM system with space-based elements, which subsequently received the official title "Strategic Defense Initiative." In our view, however, those who described it as the "Star Wars" program were far more accurate.

The president did not provide a clear definition of what the system he proposed would be like. But he declared that it was designed to make nuclear arms "impotent and obsolete" and so would remove the threat of nuclear war. In fact, that is far from true. The purpose of SDI is to achieve military superiority over the Soviet Union. In a statement to the Senate Armed Services Committee, Caspar Weinberger, then U.S. defense secretary, cynically admitted that. Here are his exact words: "If we were able to acquire a system that was efficient, and if we knew that it could make their weapons (that is, the Soviet Union's weapons . . .) impotent [not a threat], we would return to the situation where we were the only country to possess nuclear weapons."

The extremely dangerous nature of such a program was obvious right from the start. The very next day after Ronald Reagan's statement, Congressman Tom Downey declared that the president's proposal to build an ABM system in outer space "is a most horrific and absurd idea." "The president believes that lasers and beam weapons would be defensive by nature, but it is quite obvious that this is not so," another congressman, Jim Moody (D-WI), pointed out. "The introduction of more sophisticated weapons," he continued, "can lead only to the introduction of more powerful counterweapons." Another congressman, Les AuCoin (D-WI), said these words: "The president wants military superiority. But the Soviets will not stand still or allow us to achieve superiority. Instead, they will create new weapons which will in turn be capable of neutralizing space weapons."

As though summing up all of these statements, the *New York Times* wrote that "the president decided to develop research work on a new type of ABM system, despite the fact that many of his aides at the White House and the Defense Department believed that this idea had not been studied sufficiently." Valid concern was also aroused by the fact that the implementation of SDI runs counter to the 1972 Soviet-U.S. treaty on the limitation of ABM systems. It is no coincidence that even

now, in the early stages of SDI implementation, the administration is trying to circumvent its provisions by resorting to the so-called "broad interpretation" and, essentially, rejecting a number of the treaty's provisions.

The opposition to the "Star Wars" program even among U.S. legislators is evidenced by the fact that Congress is systematically reducing the administration's requests for funds to be allocated to SDI. Thus, the requests for fiscal 1988 were cut from $5.7 billion to $3.9 billion. Nor has the idea of a "broad interpretation" of the ABM treaty met with the expected support in the Senate.

Nevertheless, the United States has been carrying out intensive development in the ABM sphere throughout these five years. . . .

A considerable role is undoubtedly played here by pressure from the military-industrial corporations, which reckon on making superprofits out of implementing the program. But probably no less significant is the fact that the champions of "Star Wars" have managed to enlist considerable support by means of a forceful propaganda campaign. For the average American, who does not understand all the subtleties of foreign and military policy, the promises to safeguard the country against a possible nuclear strike with the help of a "space shield" appear very alluring. Many Americans have been enthralled by the usual illusions and stereotypes. So many people in the United

States, even those who are skeptical about SDI, deem it necessary to continue research to find out whether it is possible, from a scientific and technical viewpoint, to create a strategic defense system. What is the position today of this widely publicized program? . . . "SDI makes a nuclear war more likely," Eugene Carroll, deputy director of Washington's Center for Defense Information, emphasized, "because it pushes toward a buildup of offensive nuclear arms. And yet it is precisely this process that the United States and the Soviet Union are seeking to reverse during the Geneva talks on reducing strategic arms.". . .

Technical Problems

The U.S. press reports that SDI has also encountered a number of purely technical problems. In the opinion of U.S. specialists, its command and management programs, without which the whole system cannot function, are "suffering total failure." *Newsweek* magazine, for example, believes that "unless there is some unforeseen technological leap, SDI is threatened with gradually fading away." However, champions of "Star Wars" are seeking to give it a new boost and to achieve its unconditional implementation. Attempts are being made to technically revamp the program. Tests within the SDI framework are designed, in the opinion of its adherents, to convince skeptics of the program's efficiency and technical feasibility. . . .

Certain U.S. figures are already proposing the rejection of the ambitious plans to create a "space shield" and the reorientation of research within the SDI framework toward developing a considerably more modest system. But this is a complex issue. Thus, Senator Sam Nunn has proposed turning SDI into a "sensible defense initiative." "If we cautiously changed the thrust of our research, it could enable us to develop a limited system to counter the frightening possibility of an accidental or unsanctioned launch," Nunn declared. But champions of SDI are inclined to regard this proposal as a first step toward deploying a large-scale ABM system with space-based elements. . . .

It is still too early to draw a conclusion about how events will develop further around SDI. Its future appears rather uncertain. But there is no doubt that today it remains an adventurist undertaking with extremely dangerous consequences.

Dmitri Klimov, "Five Years of SDI: What Next?" *Krasnaya Zvezda* (*Red Star*), March 23, 1988.

The 1980s Anti–Nuclear War Movement

During the 1980s, President Ronald Reagan authorized a rapid increase in the production of a wide array of nuclear missiles, including the long-range MX Peacekeepers that carried ten nuclear warheads each. Alarmed by this unprecedented nuclear buildup, a grassroots no-nukes movement organized in cities across the country to protest the government's policy. Some officials criticized the no-nukes movement as naïve or, even pro-Communist, but George Kennan, a former diplomat and one of the key architects of U.S. nuclear policy in the 1950s, was sympathetic to the cause. In the following excerpt from his 1981 book The Nuclear Delusion: Soviet-American Relations in the Atomic Age, *Kennan defends the no-nukes movement and calls on the government to negotiate a weapons reduction treaty.*

The recent growth and gathering strength of the anti-nuclear-war movement here and in Europe is to my mind the most striking phenomenon of this beginning of the 1980s. It is all the more impressive because it is so extensively spontaneous. It has already achieved dimensions which will make it impossible, I think, for the respective governments to ignore it. It will continue to grow until something is done to meet it.

Like any great spontaneous popular movement, this one has, and must continue to have, its ragged edges, and even its dangers. It will attract the freaks and the extremists. Many of the wrong people will attach themselves to it. It will wander off in mistaken directions and become confused with other causes that are less worthy. It already shows need of leadership and of centralized organization.

But it is idle to try to stamp it, as some have done, as a Communist-inspired movement. Of course, Communists try to get into the act. Of course, they exploit the movement wherever they can. These are

George Kennan, one of the architects of nuclear policy in the 1950s, speaks out against expansion of the U.S. nuclear weapons program.

routine political tactics. But actually, I see no signs that the Communist input into this great public reaction has been of any decisive significance. . . .

[This] movement against nuclear armaments and nuclear war may be ragged and confused and disorganized, but at the heart of it lie some very fundamental and reasonable and powerful motivations: among them a growing appreciation by many people of the true horrors of a nuclear war; a determination not to see their children deprived of life, or their civilization destroyed, by a holocaust [thorough destruction] of this nature;

and finally . . . a very real exasperation with their governments for the rigidity and traditionalism that cause those governments to ignore the fundamental distinction between conventional weapons and the weapons of mass destruction and prevent them from finding, or even seriously seeking, ways of escape from the fearful trap into which the cultivation of nuclear weapons is leading us. . . .

Our government will ignore this fact at its peril. This movement is too powerful, too elementary, too deeply embedded in the natural human instinct for self-preservation, to be brushed aside. Sooner or later, and the sooner the better, all the governments on both sides of the East-West division will find themselves compelled to undertake the search for positive alternatives to the insoluble [unsolvable] dilemmas which any suicidal form of weaponry presents, and can only present.

Do Such Alternatives Exist?

Of course they do. One does not have to go far to look for them. A start could be made with deep cuts in the long-range strategic missilery. There could be a complete denuclearization of Central and Northern Europe. There could be a complete ban on nuclear testing. At the very least, one could accept a temporary freeze on the further buildup of these fantastic arsenals. None of this would undermine anyone's security.

These alternatives, obviously, are not ones that we in the West could expect to realize all by ourselves. I am not suggesting

any unilateral [one-sided] disarmament. Plainly, two . . . will have to play at this game. And even these alternatives would be only a beginning. But they would be a tremendously hopeful beginning. And what I am suggesting is that one should at least begin to explore them—and to explore them with a good will and a courage and an imagination the signs of which I fail, as yet, to detect on the part of those in Washington who have our destinies in their hands. . . .

This, then, in my opinion, is what ought to be done—what will, someday, have to be done. But for this country the change will not come easily, even in the best of circumstances. It is not something that could be accomplished from one day to the next by any simple one-time decision. What is involved in the effort to turn these things around is a fundamental and extensive change in our prevailing outlooks on a number of points, and an extensive restructuring of our entire defense posture.

We would have to begin by accepting the validity of two very fundamental appreciations [points]. The first is that there is no issue at stake in our political relations with the Soviet Union—no hope, no fear, nothing to which we aspire, nothing we would like to avoid—which could conceivably be worth a nuclear war. And the second is that there is no way in which nuclear weapons could conceivably be employed in combat that would not involve the possibility—and indeed the prohibitively high probability—of escalation into a general nuclear disaster.

If we can once get these two truths into our heads, then the next thing we will have to do is to abandon the option to which we have stubbornly clung for thirty years: the first use of nuclear weapons in any military encounter. This flows with iron logic from the two propositions I have just enunciated. First use of these weapons has long been rendered irrational by the ability of the USSR to respond in kind. The insistence on this option of first use has corrupted and vitiated our entire policy on nuclear matters ever since these weapons were first developed. I am persuaded that we shall never be able to exert a construc-

British protesters carry banners urging a halt to further development of nuclear weapons.

tive leadership in matters of nuclear arms reduction or in the problem of nuclear proliferation until this pernicious [destructive] and indefensible position is abandoned. . . .

Distortions and Exaggerations

I must go on and say that I find the view of the Soviet Union that prevails today in large portions of our governmental and journalistic establishments so extreme, so subjective, so far removed from what any sober scrutiny of external reality would reveal, that it is not only ineffective but dangerous as a guide to political action.

This endless series of distortions and oversimplifications; this systematic dehumanization of the leadership of another great country; this routine exaggeration of Moscow's military capabilities and of the supposed iniquity [evil] of Soviet intentions; this monotonous misrepresentation of the nature and the attitudes of another great people—and a long-suffering people at that, sorely tried by the vicissitudes [difficulties] of this past century; this ignoring of their pride, their hopes—yes, even of their illusions (for they have their illusions, just as we have ours; and illusions, too, deserve respect); this reckless application of the double standard to the judgment of Soviet conduct and our own; this failure to recognize, finally, the communality [commonness] of many of their problems and ours as we both move inexorably [inevitably] into the modern technological age; and this corresponding tendency to view all aspects of the relationship in terms of a supposed total and irreconcilable conflict of concerns and of aims: these, believe me, are not the marks of the maturity and discrimination one expects of the diplomacy of a great power; they are the marks of an intellectual primitivism and naivety unpardonable in a great government. . . .

Surely there is among us, at least among the majority of us, a sufficient health of the spirit, a sufficient affirmation of life, with all its joys and excitements and all its hazards and uncertainties, to permit us to slough off [ignore] this morbid preoccupation, to see it and discard it as the illness it is, to turn our attention to the real challenges and possibilities that loom beyond it, and in this way to restore to ourselves our confidence in ourselves and our hope for the future of the civilization to which we all belong.

Chapter 3

The Cold War at Home

The Cold War was more than a conflict over nuclear weapons and territory. It was also an ideological war fueled by the fear of a vastly foreign culture. Americans, in particular, feared the spread of Communist ideology, a political philosophy very different from their own. Communist governments controlled all aspects of people's lives, did not allow religious worship, and forbade free expression. For Americans used to an open society based on free speech and freedom of religion, the spread of communism represented a significant threat that had to be eliminated.

Federal Bureau of Investigation (FBI) director J. Edgar Hoover led the domestic charge against communism. As part of his campaign, Hoover kept secret files on hundreds of thousands of Americans. Among these were senators, congresspeople, writers, college professors, actors, even presidents. In the early 1950s, Hoover turned over some of this information to Wisconsin senator Joseph McCarthy, another rabid anti-Communist who vowed to cleanse the United States of the Communist threat. In a series of congressional hearings that became more like witch-hunts, McCarthy's Senate Government Operations Committee, also known as the Permanent Investigations Subcommittee, accused thousands of people of harboring Communist sympathies. Most of the accusations were baseless, but fearful Americans required little evidence of these crimes. Just an accusation was enough to ruin a suspect's life and career. Many of those brought before McCarthy's committee were subsequently fired from their jobs; shunned by former associates, these individuals found themselves pariahs in their communities.

In this atmosphere of anti-Communist hysteria, government agencies, from the FBI to the Central Intelligence Agency (CIA) to the Internal Revenue Service (IRS), began spying on Americans. Representatives of these agencies opened mail, used illegal wiretaps, and conducted smear campaigns against people accused of being Communist sympathizers. Again, most of the accusations were baseless. Many of the accused had no Communist leanings and were simply exercising political rights guaranteed by the Constitution. Anyone who questioned government policies, for example, was open to accusations of being a Communist. This widespread abuse by federal agencies was finally exposed by the U.S. Senate during the 1970s.

For the most part, the people who were targets of Hoover, McCarthy, and others were people in leadership positions. For ordinary Americans, the Communist threat centered on the possibility of a direct nuclear confrontation. This concern prompted many families to build fallout shelters, underground refuges they hoped would protect them in case of an attack. Children in schools participated in drills that had them covering their heads and ducking under their desks at the sound of an air-raid siren, also in an attempt to avoid nuclear fallout. Such tactics have since been proven to be ineffective, but they were the norm during much of the 1950s.

As the Cold War intensified, it increasingly dominated life on the home front. Politicians and civilians alike felt its effects. And as people went to jail simply for expressing unpopular ideas and government officials approved the creation of more and

deadlier nuclear weapons, some people began to wonder whether the United States was fighting against communism or emulating the tactics of a political power it professed to despise.

Joseph McCarthy (center) meets with the press and members of the Senate to suggest ways of cleansing the country of Communists.

FBI Chief Rails Against Communists

During much of the Cold War era, FBI director J. Edgar Hoover was obsessed with the idea that Communists and radicals presented a real threat to the American way of life; he included in this category political liberals, some union members, people of foreign birth, and African Americans asking for equal rights. Although the First Amendment to the Constitution guarantees freedom of speech and assembly to all citizens, Hoover argued that Communists had no such rights in America because they were spreading an ideology hostile to U.S. interests. In 1946, when the American Legion, a conservative veterans organization, presented J. Edgar Hoover with the Distinguished Service Medal, the powerful FBI chief used the opportunity to strike out against members of the American Communist Party. Although some of Hoover's statements in the following excerpt from his Distinguished Service Medal speech are exaggerations, even plainly untrue, the FBI director's views expressed in this acceptance speech helped launch a wave of anti-Communist hysteria in the 1950s.

I accept the Distinguished Service Medal of the American Legion on behalf of my associates in the Federal Bureau of Investigation who have made its achievements possible. Bulwarking the men and women of the FBI are the high hopes and expectations of the loyal Americans whom we serve. The American Legion is a great force for good in this nation. It exemplifies the tradi-

tions of our country and is living testimony to the spirit of America. I am happy to be here today to thank you of the American Legion for the great aid and assistance you have rendered the FBI over the years.

The record of your achievements is now history. Today, there is a greater need than ever before for the American Legion and its stabilizing force. We of the FBI need your help now even more than during the war years if the battle for a safe and secure America is to be won. Our enemies are massing their forces on two main fronts. One is the criminal front. Crime is increasing daily; juvenile delinquency is shocking; lawlessness is rampant. We are nearer to the days of [street] gang control than we were a year after World War I. Add to the forces that account for a serious crime every twenty seconds, day and night, the other encroaching enemy of America and we have a formidable foe. I refer to the growing menace of Communism in the United States.

During the past five years, American Communists have made their deepest inroads upon our national life. In our vaunted [well-known] tolerance for all peoples the Communist has found our "Achilles' heel" [weakness]. The American Legion represents a force which holds within its power the ability to expose the hypocrisy and ruthlessness of this foreign "ism" which has crept into our national life—an "ism" built and supported by dishonor, deceit, tyranny and a deliberate policy of falsehood.

J. Edgar Hoover argues that Communists are not entitled to freedom of speech.

It is a matter of self-preservation. The veteran who fought for America will be among the first to suffer if the Communists succeed in carrying out their diabolical [evil] plots to wreck the American way of life. The "divide and conquer" tactics did not die with [Nazi Germany leader Adolf] Hitler—they are being employed with greater skill today by American Communists with their "boring from within" strategy. Their propaganda, skillfully designed and adroitly [cleverly] executed, has been projected into practically every phase of our national life. The fact that the Communist Party in the United States claims some 100,000 members has lulled many Americans into feelings of false complacency. I would not be concerned if we were dealing with only 100,000 Communists. The Communists themselves boast that for every Party member there are ten others ready to do the Party's work. These include their satellites, their fellow-travelers and their so-called progressive and phony liberal allies. They have maneuvered themselves into positions where a few Communists control the destinies of hundreds who are either willing to be led or have been duped [tricked] into obeying the dictates [orders] of others.

"Eternal Vigilance Will Continue"

The average American working man is loyal, patriotic and law-abiding. He wants security for his family and himself. But in some [labor] unions the rank and file [common workers] find themselves between a Communist pincers, manipulated by a few leaders who have hoodwinked [tricked] and browbeaten [bullied] them into a state of submission. Communist labor leaders have sparred for time in their labor deliberations to refer matters of policy to Communist Party headquarters for clearance. In fact, resolutions have been delayed pending such approval and contemplated strikes have been postponed until adequate Communist support and backing were available.

The Communist influence has projected itself into some newspapers, magazines, books, radio and the screen. Some churches, schools, colleges and even fraternal orders have been penetrated, not with the approval of the rank and file but in spite of them. I have been pleased to observe that the Communist attempts to penetrate the American Legion have met with failure. Eternal vigilance will continue to keep your ranks free of shifty, double-crossing Communist[s]. . . .

We are rapidly reaching the time when loyal Americans must be willing to stand up and be counted. The American Communist Party, despite its claims, is not truly a political party. The Communist Party in this country is not working for the general welfare of all our people—it is working against our people. It is not interested in providing for the common defense. It has for its purpose the shackling of America and its conversion to the Godless, Communist way of life. If it were a political party its adherents could be appealed to by reason. Instead, it is a system of intrigue, actuated [driven] by fanaticism. It knows no rules of decency. Its unprincipled converts would sell America short if it would help their cause of furthering an alien way of life conceived in darkness and motivated by greed for power whose ultimate aim is the destruction of our cherished freedom. Let us no longer be misled by their sly propaganda and false preachments on civil liberty. They want civil license to do as they please and, if they get control, liberty for Americans will be but a haunted memory. For those who seek to provoke prejudice and stir up the public mind to angry resentment against our form of government are a menace to the very powers of law and order which guarantee and safeguard popular rights.

We, of this generation, have faced two great menaces in America—Fascism [as spread by the Nazis] and Communism. Both are materialistic; both are totalitarian; both are anti-religious; both are degrading and inhuman. In fact, they differ little except in name. Communism has bred Fascism and Fascism spawns Communism. Both are the antithesis [opposite] of American belief in liberty and freedom. If the peoples of other countries want Communism, let them have it, but it has no place in America. . . .

All those who stand for the American way of life must arise and defeat Red Fascism [Communism] in America by focusing upon it the spotlight of public opinion and by building up barriers of common decency through which it cannot penetrate. . . .

The men and women who defeated the Nazi brand of Fascism with bullets [during World War II] can defeat the Red brand of Fascism by raising their voices in behalf of Democracy and by exposure and denunciation of every force which weakens America. . . .

To allow America to become infected with the malignant [cancerous] growth of Communism or to be infested by crime is a breach of our trust to those who gave their lives for American principles.

Let us gird [fortify] ourselves with the determination that those basic freedoms and spiritual ideals for which so many have sacrificed so much shall not be destroyed from within.

Let us be steadfast for America, work and live for America, and eternally be on guard to defend our Constitution and our way of life against the virulent poison of Communistic ideology.

J. Edgar Hoover, speech delivered at the annual convention of the American Legion, San Francisco, California, September 30, 1946.

Truman Establishes a Loyalty Board

With dozens of powerful officials, including FBI director J. Edgar Hoover, claiming that Communists had infiltrated the U.S. government, Presi- *dent Harry Truman created the Loyalty Review Board in November 1947 to investigate individuals charged with expressing anti-American ideas. Although Truman's order attempted to be fair to those so charged, many innocent people lost their jobs and had their reputations permanently tarnished. A few even committed suicide. In the following statement, Truman spells out the duties of the Loyalty Review Board and the rights of the accused.*

I deeply appreciate the willingness of the members of the Loyalty Review Board . . . to give of their service to that Board. Their acceptance involves real personal sacrifice. At the same time, they will have the satisfaction of knowing that they are contributing to the solution of one of the most difficult problems confronting our Government today.

I believe I speak for all the people of the United States when I say that disloyal and subversive [traitorous] elements must be removed from the employ of the Government. We must not, however, permit employees of the Federal Government to be labeled as disloyal or potentially disloyal to their Government when no valid basis exists for arriving at such a conclusion. The overwhelming majority of Federal employees are loyal citizens who are giving conscientiously of their energy and skills to the United States. I do not want them to fear they are the objects of any "witch hunt." They are not being spied upon; they are not being restricted in their activities. They have nothing to fear from the loyalty program, since every effort has been made to guarantee full protection to those who are suspected of disloyalty. Rumor, gossip, or suspicion will not be sufficient to lead to the dismissal of an employee for disloyalty.

Any person suspected of disloyalty must be served with a written notice of the charges against him in sufficient detail to enable him to prepare his defense. In some unusual situations security considerations may not allow full disclosure.

It would have been possible for the Government to remove disloyal persons merely by serving them with the charges against them and giving them an opportu-

nity to answer those charges. I realize fully, however, the stigma attached to a removal for disloyalty. Accordingly, I have ordered the agencies of the Government, except where a few agencies find it necessary to exercise extraordinary powers granted to them by the Congress, to give hearings to persons who are charged with disloyalty.

Loyalty boards are being set up in each agency for this purpose. They are definitely not "kangaroo" [false] courts. The person-

---

President Harry Truman describes a government effort to expose those suspected of harboring anti-American ideas.

nel of these boards is being carefully selected by the head of each agency to make sure that they are judicious in temperament and fair-minded. Hearings before the boards will be conducted so as to establish all pertinent facts and to accord the suspected employee every possible opportunity to present his defense. The employee is to be given the right to be accompanied by counsel or a representative of his own choosing.

After the hearing has been completed the loyalty board in each department can recommend the retention or the dismissal of an employee. But the matter does not rest there. The employee may appeal the findings of the loyalty board to the head of the department, who can either approve or disapprove the board's recommendations.

If the head of the department orders the dismissal of the employee, he has still another avenue of appeal: namely, to the Loyalty Review Board. . . . This Board is composed of outstanding citizens of the United States. These citizens have no ax to grind. They will not be concerned with personalities. Their judgment will be as detached as is humanly possible. . . .

I am looking to the Federal Bureau of Investigation for the conduct of all loyalty investigations which may be necessary in connection with the operation of the program.

I am looking to the Loyalty Review Board to develop standards for the conduct of hearings and the consideration of cases within the various departments and agencies. . . . [The] Board should make sure that there is complete understanding of and adherence to these standards in all the departments and agencies.

The question of standards is of deep concern to me. Under the Executive order inaugurating this program, provision has been made, for example, for furnishing to the Loyalty Review Board by the Attorney General the name of each foreign or domestic organization, association, movement, group, or combination of persons which he, after appropriate investigation and determination, has designated as totalitarian, fascist, communist, or subversive. . . .

This provision of the order has been interpreted by some to mean that any person who at any time happened to belong to one of these organizations would automatically be dismissed from the employ of the Federal Government. . . .

Membership in an organization is simply one piece of evidence which may or may not be helpful in arriving at a conclusion as to the action which is to be taken in a particular case.

The Government has a great stake in these loyalty proceedings. The Government, as the largest employer in the United States, must be the model of a fair employer. It must guarantee that the civil rights of all employees of the Government shall be protected properly and adequately. It is in this spirit that the loyalty program will be enforced.

Harry S. Truman, announcement of the establishment of a federal Loyalty Review Board, November 14, 1947.

On Trial for Communist Beliefs

In the early 1950s, Americans who espoused Communist ideology could expect to be fired from their jobs, evicted from their homes, and even imprisoned. Steve Nelson, a former member of the Communist Party, was one such American. Nelson was arrested in Pittsburgh, Pennsylvania, on August 31, 1950, under a little-used state law against sedition, that is, using language to incite rebellion against government authority. Although the law was plainly unconstitutional, Nelson could not find a single lawyer to represent him. Most attorneys assumed their careers would be ruined if they took on such a case during a time of widespread anti-Communist hysteria. In addition, the judge presiding over the case was a member of the anti-Communist organization that had called for Nelson's arrest, a clear conflict of interest and another legal violation. In the following excerpt from his 1981 book Steve Nelson: American Radical, *Nelson recalls the experience that ended with his receiving a twenty-year sentence simply for advocating unpopular beliefs. Nelson served several years in prison before the U.S. Supreme Court overturned his conviction in 1956.*

[I was] charged with attempting to overthrow by force and violence the government of Pennsylvania and the United States under the 1919 Pennsylvania Sedition Act. Initially designed to deter labor organizing, the act had been a dead letter [unused] since the 1926 prosecution of a handful of workers from Jones and Laughlin's [steel] works. Why then were we suddenly arrested and charged with violation of it?

In the first place, the federal government was not the force that came after us. . . . Ours was a state charge all the way and it was the result of local conditions and personalities. . . .

All our efforts to get a lawyer failed. Margaret [Nelson's wife] and various friends saw over eighty in Pittsburgh who said they were too busy or that they didn't practice criminal law. Some frankly admitted that they didn't want to become another Schlesinger, the local progressive attorney who had been, at one time or another in 1950 and 1951, arrested, brought up for disbarment, and held in contempt of court, all because of his politics and whom he defended. Upon my return to Pittsburgh, I visited more than twenty-five lawyers myself and wrote to fifty others out of town. Some are willing but unable to go to court without a delay of several months. Most simply refused.

December 3 arrived, and the trial was scheduled to start. I was still without counsel. . . . I told all this to Judge Harry Montgomery and asked for a postponement. He replied that there had already been too many delays, and that the trial would start. I pointed out to him that every racketeer [career criminal] could and did get postponements. But there would be no more "dilly-dallying," as the judge told me. I demanded that doctors be appointed to examine me, and he complied, appointing them himself. . . .

I tried my last card. "Your Honor, since you apparently don't believe that I cannot get an attorney in this city, I request that you appoint a panel of attorneys with whom I can discuss the case and see if I can get one to defend me."

He hesitated but gave me the names of four lawyers who I could try to see, "but I should be prepared to go to trial tomorrow morning." I protested that no attorney could be ready to go to trial in one day. He must have other clients, whom he could not drop, and he must have time to become familiar with the case. The judge, however, refused to reconsider.

Still, I thought any lawyer was better than none. That night was a busy one. I interviewed three of the attorneys on the list, but they were unacceptable. The fourth, whom I located fifteen minutes before court opened, was only interested in his fee of fifty dollars a day.

Court then began, and Judge Montgomery asked me if I was ready to proceed. I explained that I had no attorney, but that there were three willing to represent me if they could get thirty to sixty days' time. The judge pointed out that he had done his duty by suggesting a panel, and that I was actually refusing everybody he had recommended. He denied me any more time. The trial would proceed the next day, and I was to be my own lawyer.

That night I sat up looking over old cases, trying to become a lawyer. I knew that I could begin by filing certain motions, and I asked the judge for time to do

so. He gave me fifteen minutes to write them up and present them. Margaret and I scribbled furiously and handed them over, but he hardly glanced at them. My final motion stunned the judge. I demanded that he disqualify himself because of his deep participation with those who had been behind my arrest and trial. . . . I asked him if it wasn't a fact that he was one of the founders of Americans Battling

Here, in the Allegheny County courthouse, Steve Nelson was convicted of inciting rebellion against the U.S. government.

Communism, which had demanded my arrest and circulated propaganda against me. He admitted that he was one of the officers, but "at the present time, inactive," and he refused to disqualify himself. . . .

The trial ended in late January 1952. For a few months we all remained free on bail and motions for appeals to both trials were filed. On June 26, 1952, our motion for a new trial was denied, and we were placed in the Allegheny county jail. On July 10, we appeared before Judge Montgomery and he pronounced sentence of twenty years imprisonment, court costs and $10,000 in fines—the maximum.

I was pretty upset when I heard him say twenty years, even though I knew it was coming. I think I was ready to cry. I recall looking back over my shoulder as I was led away and seeing Margaret and a few others crying. I felt very helpless. When I was put in a cell, the other men asked what I got. When I said "twenty years," one of them remarked "Holy shit!" and the others just shook their heads. Then one guy said, "You're not going to serve it, Nelson." I don't know why he said it, but it did me a lot of good.

Steve Nelson, James Barrett and Bob Ruck, *American Radical.* Pittsburgh, PA: University of Pittsburgh Press, 1981. Copyright (c) 1981 by Steve Nelson, James Barrett and Bob Ruck. Reproduced by permission.

Rosenbergs Accused of Passing Atomic Bomb Secrets

In the late 1940s, after the Soviet Union exploded its first atomic bomb, Julius and Ethel Rosenberg, *a married couple from New York City, were arrested for allegedly giving the U.S.S.R. secret atomic bomb plans stolen from the United States. The couple was charged with espionage, but the Rosenbergs steadfastly denied that they were Soviet spies. Their arrest caused a media sensation. As their trial, conviction, and appeals wound through the U.S. courts, the Rosenberg case generated worldwide publicity and an outcry for clemency because the government's case lacked any real proof of the couple's guilt. One group in particular, the National Committee to Secure Justice in the Rosenberg Case (NCSJRC), an organization formed to free the couple, worked especially hard for their release. Despite the efforts of this group and others, the Rosenbergs were executed in 1953. The following excerpt is from a booklet printed by the NCSJRC and offered as evidence of the Rosenbergs' innocence.*

On April 5, 1951, Julius Rosenberg and his wife Ethel were sentenced to die in the electric chair, having been convicted on a charge of conspiracy to spy on behalf of the Soviet Union.

The Rosenbergs have unswervingly maintained their innocence from the day of their arrest. When Ethel Rosenberg was taken to the Sing Sing death house [death row], she declared:

"We said and we say again that we are victims of the grossest type of political frame-up ever known in America."

On February 25, 1952, the U.S. Circuit Court of Appeals upheld the verdict and the sentences in a shocking decision that held, among other things, that persons could be considered disposed to commit es-

pionage by virtue of their political or social views. The defendants' attorneys will appeal the case to the Supreme Court.

Thousands of people, among them many eminent public figures, do not believe the Rosenbergs guilty or that their trial was a fair one. Thousands more, who have grave doubts of their guilt, are horrified at the death sentence.

A number of these citizens have formed the National Committee to Secure Justice in the Rosenberg Case, and many times their number have contributed money and time

Julius and Ethel Rosenberg are transported to prison after being convicted of espionage.

to make new appeals possible and to bring the case, with its far-flung implications, to the public.

Ethel and Julius Rosenberg, until their arrest, led the life of every-day people, struggling for a livelihood and education, and hoping that their two young sons, aged nine and four, would be spared the hardships familiar to the parents. . . .

The Indictment

The indictment charged the Rosenbergs with initiating a conspiracy during 1944, the last year of the war against nazism, to transmit information "relating to the national defense of the United States" to the Soviet Union.

The prosecutor however, went far beyond the indictment, charged that the Rosenbergs had given the Soviet Union the "secret" of the atom bomb, and attempted to create the impression that the Rosenbergs were "Communists," holding allegedly "subversive" [corrupt] views, and therefore disposed to commit espionage. He further attempted to impress the jury that a verdict of "innocent" would be tantamount [equal] to repudiation [rejection] of our government's foreign policy.

The Prosecution's Case

Before the trial the prosecutor announced that he would call 118 witnesses, among them top scientists Dr. J. Robert Oppenheimer, Dr. Harold C. Urey; Gen. Leslie R. Groves, head of the atom bomb project during the war; agents of the Federal Bureau of Investigation; alleged associates of the Rosenbergs in the "conspiracy"; and two "star" witnesses. All witnesses were supposed to give evidence of Rosenberg's alleged spy activities. . . .

Two witnesses, David and Ruth Greenglass, were both, according to the prosecutor, and their own statements, involved in the alleged conspiracy, but as a result of their testimony . . . Ruth was never brought to trial, and her husband got off with a 15 year sentence.

The government's entire case is based on the Greenglass's uncorroborated [unsupported] testimony, a fact conceded by the Court of Appeals, which in upholding the convictions declared that without the testimony of the Greenglasses, "the conviction could not stand." The prosecutor produced 32 exhibits as "documentary evidence." Not one of these documents, by the prosecutor's own admission, connected the Rosenbergs with a conspiracy to commit espionage. In fact, only two of the documents had any link whatever to the Rosenbergs.

One was a collection can issued by the [Communist-based] Spanish Refugee Appeal, the other was a nominating petition, signed by Ethel, for Peter V. Cacchione, a successful Communist candidate for the City Council of New York.

The prosecutor filled the overwhelming bulk of his case with persistent insinuations that the Rosenbergs were Communists, the U.S. monopoly of the atom bomb was important to world peace, and that war with the Soviet Union was virtually inevitable.

The Star Witnesses

David Greenglass, brother of Ethel Rosenberg, and his wife Ruth, were the star witnesses against the Rosenbergs. Both admitted that they had committed espionage for which they received money and for which both could be given the death penalty.

David Greenglass was arrested in June and indicted in July 1950. He was held on $100,000 bail, placed in solitary confinement, and visited for hours at a time by the FBI. . . .

The Greenglass' uncorroborated testimony was the only evidence presented that the Rosenbergs had conspired to steal the atom-bomb secret. Their testimony in respect to the Rosenbergs was solely oral, and no documents or other proofs linking the Rosenbergs to espionage were introduced. No witnesses were called to substantiate [prove] any conversations on espionage that allegedly took place between the Greenglasses and the Rosenbergs. David Greenglass testified that relying solely on his memory of snatches [bits] of overheard conversation at the atom-bomb project at Los Alamos [New Mexico], and his remembrance of details of blueprints which had been shown to him as part of his work as a machinist, he had drawn up an elaborate sketch of the atom bomb, together with twelve pages of written material, which he allegedly conveyed as a description of the bomb to Rosenberg.

The following are Greenglass' actual qualifications for this impressive feat:

1) experience as an ordinary machinist in both army and civilian life;

2) a high school education, plus 8 technical courses at Brooklyn Polytechnic Institute, in all 8 of which he admitted he was graded "failure";

3) an admission that he was ignorant of the formulae governing component parts of the atom bomb, and that he had never taken courses or read books on such essential subjects as elementary, differential or advanced calculus, thermodynamics, quantum mechanics, nuclear or atomic physics. . . .

The Death Sentence

In imposing the death sentence against Ethel and Julius Rosenberg, Judge Irving Kaufman said that they had "altered the course of history to the disadvantage of our country . . . we have evidence of your treachery around us every day . . . I believe your conduct has already caused, in my opinion, the Communist aggression in Korea, with resultant casualties exceeding 50,000 and who knows but that millions more of innocent people may pay the price of your treason."

From the Judge's comments, it appears that he sentenced the Rosenbergs to death for crimes with which they were not at all charged. They were neither accused of treason nor was any evidence brought in linking them in any way to the instigation of any wars, past, present, or future. But the Judge's comments, and the death sentence, like the jury's verdict, is in line with the prosecution's inability to bring in convincing proof that the Rosenbergs conspired to commit espionage, substituting, instead, inflammatory and reckless charges that had nothing to do with the case.

The Taint of Anti-Semitism

Shortly after the trial was over the prosecutor, although Jewish, was severely reprimanded by a United States Court of

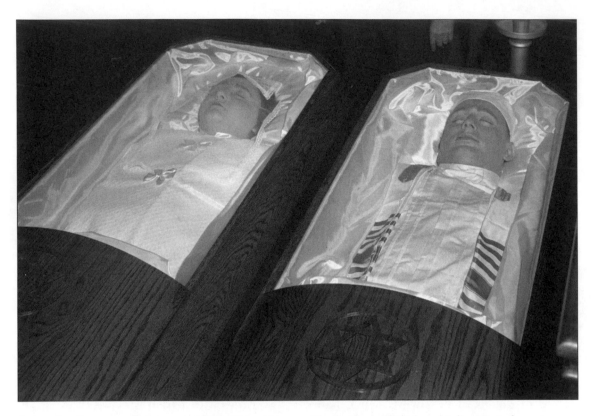

The bodies of Ethel and Julius Rosenberg are placed on view after their execution.

Appeals for practicing anti-Semitism in another case. This grave charge is bolstered by the fact that the Rosenberg trial, in a city whose population is one-third Jewish, proceeded without a single Jewish juror due to challenges by the prosecution.

Here are comments from the Jewish press:

THE DAY: "The death sentence imposed by Judge Kaufman left the feeling that precisely because he is a Jew did he go to an extreme and deal judgment with a heavy hand . . . that Judge Kaufman is a Jew has perhaps unconsciously motivated him to issue a sentence which, in the opinion of many, is considered to be unjust and brutal."

DAILY FORWARD: "Too horrible . . . every Jew feels the same way."

CHICAGO SENTINEL, an Anglo-Jewish paper, in a column on Feb. 7, 1952 by Rabbi G. George Fox, one of the most widely known Rabbis in the mid-west, an eminent scholar and author: "I am certain that Judge Kaufman's decision will be found unjust, if not illegal."

Conclusions

1) The Rosenbergs were convicted on unsubstantial and incredible evidence.

2) The prosecution prejudiced and inflamed the jury by bringing in extraneous [unrelated] issues in every phase of the trial.

3) The suspicion of anti-Semitism taints the entire trial.

When it is borne in mind that Ethel and Julius Rosenberg were ordinary folk like the vast majority of us, that they were not leaders of any political or social or economic movements, it becomes clear that a new danger faces this vast majority, the danger that past or present or future views on social issues may become the basis for wild accusations, imprisonment, and even death. That is why it is in the interest of all Americans, regardless of their beliefs and creeds, to make certain that justice is done in the Rosenberg Case.

National Committee to Secure Justice in the Rosenberg Case, "Investigation of Communist Activities," Norton Exhibit No. 2, fact sheet submitted to the House Committee on Un-American Activities. Washington, DC: U.S. Government Printing Office, 1955.

Influence of the Military-Industrial Complex

Dwight Eisenhower was a World War II hero who, as president, oversaw a huge increase in military spending during the 1950s. In January 1961, after completing two successful terms, Eisenhower gave a farewell address to the nation. In the address, he warned Americans of the growing power and influence of the weapons industry, or military-industrial complex. Commenting that the United States had never had a perma-nent arms-manufacturing industry in its nearly two-hundred-year history, the president noted that the military-industrial complex now exerted powerful influence in almost every city, state, and federal government office. In the following excerpt from the speech, Eisenhower acknowledges the dangerous powers of the Soviet Union but at the same time sounds the alarm about the growing sphere of influence of the arms industry.

This evening I come to you with a message of leave-taking and farewell, and to share a few final thoughts with you, my countrymen. . . . Throughout America's adventure

President Dwight Eisenhower warns the public about the growing clout of the military weapons industry.

in free government, our basic purposes have been to keep the peace; to foster progress in human achievement, and to enhance liberty, dignity and integrity among people and among nations. To strive for less would be unworthy of a free and religious people. Any failure traceable to arrogance, or our lack of comprehension or readiness to sacrifice would inflict upon us grievous hurt both at home and abroad.

Progress toward these noble goals is persistently threatened by the conflict now engulfing the world. It commands our whole attention, absorbs our very beings. We face a hostile [Communist] ideology—global in scope, atheistic in character, ruthless in purpose, and insidious [devious] in method. Unhappily the danger it poses promises to be of indefinite duration. To meet it successfully, there is called for, not so much the emotional and transitory sacrifices of crisis, but rather those which enable us to carry forward steadily, surely, and without complaint the burdens of a prolonged and complex struggle—with liberty the stake. Only thus shall we remain, despite every provocation, on our charted course toward permanent peace and human betterment. . . . A vital element in keeping the peace is our military establishment. Our arms must be mighty, ready for instant action, so that no potential aggressor may be tempted to risk his own destruction.

Our military organization today bears little relation to that known by any of my predecessors in peacetime, or indeed by the fighting men of World War II or Korea.

The Military-Industrial Complex

Until the latest of our world conflicts, the United States had no armaments industry. American makers of plowshares could, with time and as required, make swords as well. But now we can no longer risk emergency improvisation of national defense; we have been compelled to create a permanent armaments industry of vast proportions. Added to this, three and a half million men and women are directly engaged in the defense establishment. We annually spend on military security more than the net income of all United States corporations.

This conjunction of an immense military establishment and a large arms industry is new in the American experience. The total influence—economic, political, even spiritual—is felt in every city, every State house, every office of the Federal government. We recognize the imperative need for this development. Yet we must not fail to comprehend its grave implications. Our toil, resources and livelihood are all involved; so is the very structure of our society.

In the councils of government, we must guard against the acquisition of unwarranted influence, whether sought or unsought, by the military-industrial complex. The potential for the disastrous rise of misplaced power exists and will persist.

We must never let the weight of this combination endanger our liberties or democratic processes. We should take nothing for granted. Only an alert and knowledgeable citizenry can compel the proper meshing of the huge industrial and military machinery of defense with our peaceful methods and goals, so that security and liberty may prosper together. . . . Another factor in maintaining balance involves the element of time. As we peer into society's future, we—you and I, and our government—must avoid the impulse to live only for today, plundering, for our own ease and convenience, the precious resources of tomorrow. We cannot mortgage the material assets of our grandchildren without risking the loss also of their political and spiritual heritage. We want democracy to survive for all generations to come, not to become the insolvent phantom of tomorrow.

Down the long lane of the history yet to be written America knows that this world of ours, ever growing smaller, must avoid becoming a community of dreadful fear and hate, and be, instead, a proud confederation of mutual trust and respect. . . .

So—in this my last good night to you as your President—I thank you for the many opportunities you have given me for public service in war and peace. I trust that in that service you find some things worthy; as for the rest of it, I know you will find ways to improve performance in the future. . . .

To all the peoples of the world, I once more give expression to America's prayerful and continuing aspiration:

We pray that peoples of all faiths, all races, all nations, may have their great human needs satisfied; that those now denied opportunity shall come to enjoy it to the full; that all who yearn for freedom may ex-perience its spiritual blessings; that those who have freedom will understand, also, its heavy responsibilities; that all who are insensitive to the needs of others will learn charity; that the scourges of poverty, disease and ignorance will be made to disappear from the earth, and that, in the goodness of time, all peoples will come to live together in a peace guaranteed by the binding force of mutual respect and love.

Dwight D. Eisenhower, farewell address to the American people, broadcast and televised January 17, 1961.

Government Agencies Spy on Americans

In 1975 and 1976, a committee in the U.S. Senate (called the Church Committee because it was led by Senator Frank Church, a Democrat from Idaho) revealed that the FBI, CIA, National Security Agency (NSA), IRS, and other federal agencies had been illegally spying on and harassing Americans for decades. The Church Committee made these deductions after taking testimony from hundreds of people and collecting hundreds of thousands of files from various federal agencies. The Church Committee issued fourteen reports that detailed a widespread, illegal pattern of abuse by these agencies against Americans engaging in legal activities such as protesting the Vietnam War or marching in civil rights demonstrations. In addition to costing millions of dollars, these government spy operations violated the constitutional rights of hundreds of thousands of Americans. The following excerpt from the Church Committee report offers details of the activities conducted by the CIA, FBI, and IRS.

Americans have rightfully been concerned since before World War II about the dangers of hostile foreign agents likely to commit acts of espionage. Similarly, the violent acts of political terrorists can seriously endanger the rights of Americans. Carefully focused intelligence investigations can help prevent such acts.

But too often intelligence has lost this focus and domestic intelligence activities have invaded individual privacy and violated the rights of lawful assembly and political expression. . . .

[The Church Committee has] examined three types of "intelligence" activities affecting the rights of American citizens.

The first is intelligence collection—such as infiltrating groups with informants, wiretapping, or opening letters. The second is dissemination of material which has been collected. The third is covert action designed to disrupt and discredit the activities of groups and individuals deemed a threat to the social order. . . .

This Committee has examined . . . the collection of intelligence about the political advocacy and actions and the private lives of American citizens. That information has been used covertly to discredit the

Senator Frank Church reveals details of illegal government spying on Americans.

ideas advocated and to "neutralize" the actions of their proponents. . . .

Our investigation has confirmed that. . . . segments of our Government, in their attitudes and action, adopt tactics unworthy of a democracy, and occasionally reminiscent of the tactics of totalitarian regimes. We have seen a consistent pattern in which programs initiated with limited goals, such as preventing criminal violence or identifying foreign spies, were expanded to what witnesses characterized as "vacuum cleaners", sweeping in information about lawful activities of American citizens. . . .

"Break Up Marriages, Disrupt Meetings"

Too many people have been spied upon by too many Government agencies and too much information has [been] collected. The Government has often undertaken the secret surveillance of citizens on the basis of their political beliefs, even when those beliefs posed no threat of violence or illegal acts on behalf of a hostile foreign power. The Government, operating primarily through secret informants, but also using other intrusive techniques such as wiretaps, microphone "bugs", surreptitious [secret] mail opening, and break-ins, has swept in vast amounts of information about the personal lives, views, and associations of American citizens. Investigations of groups deemed potentially dangerous—and even of groups suspected of associating with potentially dangerous organizations—have continued for decades, despite the fact that those groups did not engage in unlawful activity. Groups and individuals have been harassed and disrupted because of their political views and their lifestyles. Investigations have been based upon vague standards whose breadth made excessive collection inevitable. Unsavory and vicious tactics have been employed—including anonymous attempts to break up marriages, disrupt meetings, ostracize persons from their professions, and provoke target groups into rivalries that might result in deaths. Intelligence agencies have served the political and personal objectives of presidents and other high officials. While the agencies often committed excesses in response to pressure from high officials in the Executive branch and Congress, they also occasionally initiated improper activities and then concealed them from officials whom they had a duty to inform.

Governmental officials—including those whose principal duty is to enforce the law—have violated or ignored the law over long periods of time and have advocated and defended their right to break the law. . . .

United States intelligence agencies have investigated a vast number of American citizens and domestic organizations. FBI headquarters alone has developed over 500,000 domestic intelligence files, and these have been augmented [added to] by additional files at FBI Field Offices. The FBI opened 65,000 of these domestic intelligence files in 1972 alone. In fact, substantially more individuals and groups are subject to intelligence scrutiny than the number of files would appear to indicate, since typically, each domestic intelligence file contains information on more than one individual or group, and this information is readily retrievable through the FBI General Name Index.

The number of Americans and domestic groups caught in the domestic intelligence net is further illustrated by the following statistics:

—Nearly a quarter of a million first class letters were opened and photographed in the United States by the CIA between 1953–1973, producing a CIA computerized index of nearly one and one-half million names.

—At least 130,000 first class letters were opened and photographed by the FBI between 1940–1966 in eight U.S. cities.

—Some 300,000 individuals were indexed in a CIA computer system and separate files were created on approximately 7,200 Americans and over 100 domestic groups during the course of [the CIA operation].

—Millions of private telegrams sent from, to, or through the United States were obtained by the National Security Agency from 1947 to 1975 under a secret arrangement with three United States telegraph companies.

—An estimated 100,000 Americans were the subjects of United States Army intelligence files created between the mid-1960's and 1971.

—Intelligence files on more than 11,000 individuals and groups were created by the Internal Revenue Service between 1969 and 1973 and tax investigations were started on the basis of political rather than tax criteria.

—At least 26,000 individuals were at one point catalogued on an FBI list of persons to be rounded up in the event of a "national emergency."

Intelligence agencies have collected vast amounts of information about the intimate details of citizens' lives and about their participation in legal and peaceful political activities. The targets of intelligence activity have included political adherents of the right and the left, ranging from activist to casual supporters. Investigations have been directed against proponents of racial causes and women's rights, outspoken apostles [supporters] of nonviolence and racial harmony; establishment politicians; religious groups; and advocates of new life styles.

U.S. Senate, *Final Report of the Select Committee to Study Governmental Operations with Respect to Intelligence Activities,* Book II, 94th Cong., 2nd sess., 1976.

Chapter 4

Foreign Entanglements

Even though they had assembled massive arsenals of nuclear weapons, the United States and the Soviet Union could not fight a direct war; the capability of each side to inflict heavy casualties on the other precluded that. They did come to blows indirectly, however. Throughout the Cold War, the superpowers faced off in third-world countries whose citizens were often divided in their support of democracy and communism.

The first such war took place on a small Asian peninsula. In 1945, at the end of World War II, the nation of Korea was divided into two zones along the 38th parallel. The United States took control of the southern half, called South Korea, and the Soviet Union took control of the northern half, called North Korea. The Americans and the Soviets ruled their respective halves until 1949, when both ended their occupations. The countries they left behind, however, were vastly different in military strength. The Soviets left the North Kore-

ans weapons and a well-trained army; the United States left little weaponry behind.

In 1950, Communist North Korea invaded democratic South Korea. In response, the United Nations called on the United States to lead an international military force to stop the invasion. This force included small contingents of British, Canadian, Australian, and Turkish troops, but American soldiers made up most of the army.

For three years, the superpowers battled to achieve their objectives in Korea; the North Koreans wanted to take control of both halves, and the Americans wanted to repel the invading army. Initially, it looked like the North Koreans might win; they pushed the Americans all the way to the tip of South Korea. But under the leadership of American general Douglas MacArthur, the United States responded by driving the Communists back into northern territory and ultimately to the country's border with China. That maneuver troubled

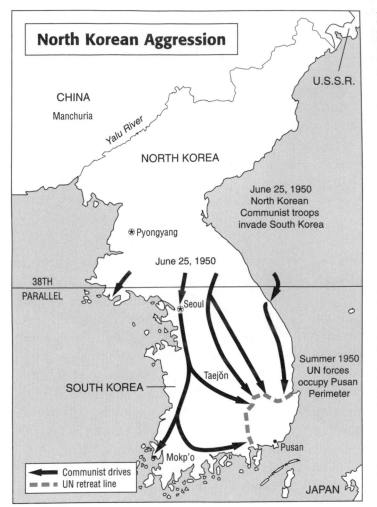

North Korean Aggression

CHINA

Manchuria

Yalu River

U.S.S.R.

NORTH KOREA

June 25, 1950
North Korean
Communist troops
invade South Korea

⊛ Pyongyang

June 25, 1950

38TH
PARALLEL

⊛ Seoul

Summer 1950
UN forces
occupy Pusan
Perimeter

Taejŏn

SOUTH KOREA

Mokp'o

• Pusan

Communist drives

UN retreat line

JAPAN

the Chinese, who worried that the Americans would invade them next. As a result, Chinese leader Mao Tse-tung sent his own troops into Korea to aid the Communist forces.

The Korean War finally ended in a stalemate. Neither side was able to claim victory, and in 1953, the foes negotiated a cease-fire that left the country divided exactly as it had been before. The conflict claimed many lives; 36,934 Americans, 1.3 million South Koreans, 500,000 North Koreans, and 1 million Chinese were killed.

Meanwhile, trouble was brewing in the Southeast Asian country of Vietnam. A French colony for decades, Vietnam had been fighting for independence since the 1930s. In 1945, Vietnamese leader and Communist Ho Chi Minh took advantage of the chaos World War II wrought and declared Vietnam an independent nation. When the French tried to retake control of Vietnam in 1947, war broke out between the Communist Vietnamese and the U.S.-aided French. The French gave up the fighting in 1954, and Vietnam, like Korea, was divided into northern and southern halves. Ho Chi Minh and the Communists, backed by the Soviet Union, took control of the North. The United States took control of the South. Initially sending only military advisers to aid the South Vietnamese, the United States got more and more involved in the fighting as the 1950s and 1960s wore on. At the height of U.S. involvement during the late 1960s, more than half a million American military personnel were stationed in Vietnam.

The Vietnam War proved to be the longest and most divisive conflict in American history. Although the most severe fighting took place during the late 1960s and early 1970s, American involvement in Vietnam lasted for nearly twenty years. And as the war escalated and thousands of American soldiers died (the United States lost fifty-eight thousand men), many people, particularly the college-aged students who were most likely to be drafted, became increasingly disillusioned with the fighting. Hundreds of thousands of people took to the streets in protest, calling for an end to the war. Many of these encounters turned violent; for example, four students were killed and nine wounded by national guardsmen in 1970 during a war protest at Ohio's Kent State University. Finally, in 1973, the United States withdrew from the fighting. Two years later, North Vietnam conquered the South.

Korea and Vietnam drew massive popular attention, but the United States also took part in covert, or secret, military operations against communism in other parts of the world. For example, the United States tried (but failed) to overthrow Cuba's Communist dictator Fidel Castro in 1961 by training Cuban exiles to invade the island nation. During the 1970s, the CIA gave money to ethnic groups battling a Soviet invasion of Afghanistan. And in the 1980s, the CIA trained and equipped local armies to fight Soviet-backed Communists in the Central American countries of Nicaragua and El Salvador.

All of these operations left millions dead but never led to a direct confrontation between the superpowers. Instead, the United States and the Soviet Union fought their ideological battle on the soil of faraway nations that often had little say in the reasons for war or in the outcome.

The U.S. Campaign in Korea

The Korean War was the first extended armed conflict of the Cold War. The U.S. commitment to fight communism led to military intervention in this faraway Asian nation and to more than thirty-six thousand Americans being killed in action.

Korea, following its liberation from Japan in World War II, had been hastily divided between Soviet and American occupation zones. These zones ultimately became two separate countries: North Korea, which allied itself with the Soviet Union, and South Korea, which maintained close ties with the United States. Both countries claimed jurisdiction over the whole of Korea.

On June 25, 1950, forces from communist North Korea attacked South Korea. United States president Harry S. Truman believed this attack was instigated by the Soviet Union and that the United States could not let the attack stand without a strong U.S. response. Truman explains his actions in this April 1951 address to the American people.

The Communists in [Moscow] are engaged in a monstrous conspiracy to stamp out freedom all over the world. If they were to succeed, the United States would be numbered among their principal victims. It must be clear to everyone that the United States cannot—and will not—sit idly by and await foreign conquest. The only question is: When is the best time to meet the threat and how?

The best time to meet the threat is in the beginning. It is easier to put out a fire in the beginning when it is small than after it has become a roaring blaze.

And the best way to meet the threat of aggression is for the peace-loving nations to act together. If they don't act together, they are likely to be picked off, one by one. . . .

Lesson of History

If history has taught us anything, it is that aggression anywhere in the world is a threat to peace everywhere in the world. When that aggression is supported by the cruel and selfish rulers of a powerful nation who are bent on conquest, it becomes a clear and present danger to the security and independence of every free nation.

This is a lesson that most people in this country have learned thoroughly. This is the basic reason why we joined in creating the United Nations. And since the end of World War II we have been putting that lesson into practice—we have been working with other free nations to check the aggressive designs of the Soviet Union before they can result in a third world war. . . .

The aggression against Korea is the boldest and most dangerous move the Communists have yet made.

The attack on Korea was part of a greater plan for conquering all of Asia.

I would like to read to you from a secret intelligence report which came to us after the attack. It is a report of a speech a Communist army officer in North Korea gave to a group of spies and saboteurs last May, one month before South Korea was invaded.

The report shows in great detail how this invasion was part of a carefully prepared plot. Here is part of what the Communist officer, who had been trained in Moscow, told his men: "Our forces," he said, "are scheduled to attack South Korean forces about the middle of June. . . . The coming attack on South Korea marks the first step toward the liberation of Asia."

Notice that he used the word "liberation." That is Communist double-talk meaning "conquest."

I have another secret intelligence report here. This one tells what another Communist officer in the Far East told his men several months before the invasion of Korea. Here is what he said: "In order to successfully undertake the long awaited world revolution, we must first unify Asia. . . . Java, Indochina, Malaya, India, Tibet, Thailand, Philippines, and Japan are our ultimate targets. . . . The United States is the only obstacle on our road for the liberation of all countries in southeast Asia. In other words, we must unify the people of Asia and crush the United States."

That is what the Communist leaders are telling their people, and that is what they have been trying to do. . . .

A Limited War

The question we have had to face is whether the Communist plan of conquest can be stopped without general war. Our Government and other countries associated with us in the United Nations believe that the best chance of stopping it without general war is to meet the attack in Korea and defeat it there.

That is what we have been doing. It is a difficult and bitter task. But so far it has been successful.

So far, we have prevented World War III.

So far, by fighting a limited war in Korea, we have prevented aggression from succeeding and bringing on a general war. And the ability of the whole free world to resist Communist aggression has been greatly improved.

We have taught the enemy a lesson. He has found out that aggression is not cheap or easy. Moreover, men all over the world who want to remain free have been given new courage and new hope. They know now that the champions of freedom can stand up and fight and that they will stand up and fight.

Our resolute stand in Korea is helping the forces of freedom now fighting in Indochina and other countries in that part of the world. It has already slowed down the timetable of conquest.

In Korea itself, there are signs that the enemy is building up his ground forces for a new mass offensive. We also know that there have been large increases in the enemy's available air forces.

If a new attack comes, I feel confident it will be turned back. The United Nations fighting forces are tough and able and well equipped. They are fighting for a just cause. They are proving to all the world that the principle of collective security will work. We are proud of all these forces for the magnificent job they have done against heavy odds. We pray that their efforts may succeed, for upon their success may hinge the peace of the world.

President Harry Truman (seated at left) talks with British and American officials about North Korea's invasion of South Korea.

The Communist side must now choose its course of action. The Communist rulers may press the attack against us. They may take further action which will spread the conflict. They have that choice, and with it the awful responsibility for what may follow. The Communists also have the choice of a peaceful settlement which could lead to a general relaxation of tensions in the Far East. The decision is theirs, because the forces of the United Nations will strive to limit the conflict if possible.

We do not want to see the conflict in Korea extended. We are trying to prevent a world war—not to start one. The best way to do that is to make it plain that we and the other free countries will continue to resist the attack.

But you may ask: Why can't we take other steps to punish the aggressor? Why don't we bomb Manchuria and China itself? Why don't we assist Chinese Nationalist troops to land on the mainland of China?

If we were to do these things we would be running a very grave risk of starting a general war. If that were to happen, we would have brought about the exact situation we are trying to prevent.

If we were to do these things, we would become entangled in a vast conflict on the continent of Asia and our task would become immeasurably more difficult all over the world.

What would suit the ambitions of the Kremlin better than for our military forces to be committed to a full-scale war with Red China?

It may well be that, in spite of our best efforts, the Communists may spread the war. But it would be wrong—tragically wrong—for us to take the initiative in extending the war.

Dangers Ahead

The dangers are great. Make no mistake about it. Behind the North Koreans and Chinese Communists in the front lines stand additional millions of Chinese soldiers. And behind the Chinese stand the tanks, the planes, the submarines, the soldiers, and the scheming rulers of the Soviet Union.

Our aim is to avoid the spread of the conflict.

The course we have been following is the one best calculated to avoid an all-out war. It is the course consistent with our obligation to do all we can to maintain international peace and security. Our experience in Greece and Berlin shows that it is the most effective course of action we can follow.

First of all, it is clear that our efforts in Korea can blunt the will of the Chinese Communists to continue the struggle. The United Nations forces have put up a tremendous fight in Korea and have inflicted very heavy casualties on the enemy. Our forces are stronger now than they have been before. These are plain facts which may discourage the Chinese Communists from continuing their attack.

Second, the free world as a whole is growing in military strength every day. In the United States, in Western Europe, and throughout the world, free men are alert to the Soviet threat and are building their defenses. This may discourage the Communist rulers from continuing the war in Korea—and from undertaking new acts of aggression elsewhere.

If the Communist authorities realize that they cannot defeat us in Korea, if they realize it would be foolhardy to widen the hostilities beyond Korea, then they may recognize the folly of continuing their aggression. A peaceful settlement may then be possible. The door is always open.

Then we may achieve a settlement in Korea which will not compromise the principles and purposes of the United Nations.

I have thought long and hard about this question of extending the war in Asia. I have discussed it many times with the ablest military advisers in the country. I believe with all my heart that the course we are following is the best course.

I believe that we must try to limit the war to Korea for these vital reasons: to make sure that the precious lives of our fighting men are not wasted; to see that the security of our country and the free world is not needlessly jeopardized, and to prevent a third world war.

A Struggle for Peace

I want to be clear about our military objective. We are fighting to resist an outrageous aggression in Korea. We are trying to keep the Korean conflict from spreading to other areas. But at the same time we must conduct our military activities so as to insure the security of our forces. This is essential if they are to continue the fight until the enemy abandons its ruthless attempt to destroy the Republic of Korea.

That is our military objective—to repel attack and to restore peace.

In the hard fighting in Korea, we are proving that collective action among nations is not only a high principle but a workable means of resisting aggression. Defeat of aggression in Korea may be the turning point in the world's search for a practical way of achieving peace and security.

The struggle of the United Nations in Korea is a struggle for peace.

The free nations have united their strength in an effort to prevent a third world war.

That war can come if the Communist rulers want it to come. But this Nation and its allies will not be responsible for its coming.

We do not want to widen the conflict. We will use every effort to prevent that disaster. And in so doing we know that we are following the great principles of peace, freedom, and justice.

Harry S. Truman, address to the American people about intervention in Korea, *Department of State Bulletin*, April 11, 1951.

Vietnam Declares Independence

The Vietnamese people had been fighting for independence from France since the 1930s. During World War II, Germany occupied France, and Japan, a Germany ally, took control of Vietnam. On September 2, 1945, two weeks before the Japanese lost the war, charismatic Vietnamese leader Ho Chi Minh took advantage of Japan's imminent defeat and declared national independence for his country. In the following excerpt, Ho quotes from the American Declaration of Independence, hoping to win the sympathy and loyalty of the U.S. government. He also lists the harmful effects that eighty years of colonialism had on Vietnam. Although the Vietnamese leader invoked democratic ideals in this speech, leaders in the United States believed that his government was backed by Communists and worried that after gaining a foothold in Vietnam, the Soviets would go on to conquer all of Southeast Asia.

"All men are created equal. They are endowed by their Creator with certain inalienable rights; among these are Life, Liberty, and the pursuit of Happiness."

This immortal statement was made in the Declaration of Independence of the United States of America in 1776. In a broader sense, this means: All the peoples on the earth are equal from birth, all the peoples have a right to live, to be happy and free.

The Declaration of the French Revolution made in 1791 on the Rights of Man and the Citizen also states: "All men are born free and with equal rights, and must always remain free and have equal rights."

Those are undeniable truths.

Nevertheless, for more than eighty years, the French imperialists, abusing the

Ho Chi Minh declared independence for Vietnam shortly before Japan's defeat in World War II.

standard of Liberty, Equality, and Fraternity [brotherhood], have violated our Fatherland and oppressed our fellow-citizens. They have acted contrary to the ideals of humanity and justice.

In the field of politics, they have deprived our people of every democratic liberty.

They have enforced inhuman laws; they have set up three distinct political regimes in the North, the Center and the South of Vietnam in order to wreck our national unity and prevent our people from being united.

They have built more prisons than schools. They have mercilessly slain our patriots; they have drowned our uprisings in rivers of blood. . . .

To weaken our race they have forced us to use opium [a drug] and alcohol.

In the field of economics, they have fleeced [robbed] us to the backbone, impoverished our people, and devastated our land.

They have robbed us of our rice fields, our mines, our forests, and our raw materials. They have monopolized the issuing of bank-notes and the export trade.

They have invented numerous unjustifiable taxes and reduced our people, especially our peasantry, to a state of extreme poverty.

They have hampered the prospering of our national bourgeoisie [middle class]; they have mercilessly exploited our workers.

In the autumn of 1940, when the Japanese Fascists violated Indochina's territory to establish new bases in their fight against the Allies, the French imperialists went down on their bended knees and handed over our country to them.

Thus, from that date, our people were subjected to the double yoke of the French and the Japanese. Their [Vietnamese] sufferings and miseries increased. The result was that from the end of last year to the beginning of this year, from Quang Tri province to the North of Vietnam, more

than two million of our fellow-citizens died from starvation. On March 9, the French troops were disarmed by the Japanese. The French colonialists either fled or surrendered showing that not only were they incapable of "protecting" us, but that, in the span of five years, they had twice sold our country to the Japanese.

Committed to Fight

On several occasions before March 9, the Vietminh League [League for Vietnamese Independence] urged the French to ally themselves with it against the Japanese. Instead of agreeing to this proposal, the French colonialists so intensified their terrorist activities against the Vietminh members that before fleeing they massacred a great number of our political prisoners detained at Yen Bay and Caobang.

Notwithstanding all this, our fellow-citizens have always manifested toward the French a tolerant and humane attitude. Even after the Japanese putsch [takeover] of March [1940], the Vietminh League helped many Frenchmen to cross the frontier, rescued some of them from Japanese jails, and protected French lives and property.

From the autumn of 1940, our country had in fact ceased to be a French colony and had become a Japanese possession.

After the Japanese had surrendered to the Allies, our whole people rose to regain our national sovereignty and to found the Democratic Republic of Vietnam.

The truth is that we have wrested our independence from the Japanese and not from the French.

The French have fled, the Japanese have capitulated [been defeated], Emperor Bao Dai [the Japanese-backed ruler] has abdicated. Our people have broken the chains which for nearly a century have fettered [restrained] them and have won independence for the Fatherland. Our people at the same time have overthrown the monarchic regime that has reigned supreme for dozens of centuries. In its place has been established the present Democratic Republic.

For these reasons, we, members of the Provisional Government, representing the whole Vietnamese people, declare that from now on we break off all relations of a colonial character with France; we repeal all the international obligation that France has so far subscribed to on behalf of Vietnam and we abolish all the special rights the French have unlawfully acquired in our Fatherland.

The whole Vietnamese people, animated by a common purpose, are determined to fight to the bitter end against any attempt by the French colonialists to reconquer their country.

We are convinced that the Allied nations which . . . have acknowledged the principles of self-determination and equality of nations, will not refuse to acknowledge the independence of Vietnam.

A people who have courageously opposed French domination for more than eight years, a people who have fought side by side with the Allies against the Fascists during these last years, such a people must be free and independent.

For these reasons, we, members of the Provisional Government of the Democratic Republic of Vietnam, solemnly declare to the world that Vietnam has the right to be a free and independent country—and in fact is so already. The entire Vietnamese people are determined to mobilize all their physical and mental strength, to sacrifice their lives and property in order to safeguard their independence and liberty.

Ho Chi Minh, Vietnam Declaration of Independence, September 2, 1945.

The CIA Tries to Assassinate Castro

Between 1960 and 1965, the CIA concocted several plots to assassinate Cuban dictator Fidel Castro. During the mid-1970s, a Senate probe into CIA abuses uncovered these top secret conspiracies and exposed them to the world. The Senate's report, excerpted below, reveals the many methods the CIA tried, including working with criminals in the Mafia, trying to make Castro's beard fall out to humiliate him, and attempting to spray him with hallucinogenic drugs before an important speech.

We [the Senate] have found concrete evidence of at least eight plots involving the CIA to assassinate [Cuban leader] Fidel Castro from 1960 to 1965. Although some of the assassination plots did not advance beyond the stage of planning and preparation, one plot, involving the use of underworld figures, reportedly twice progressed to the point of sending poison pills to Cuba and dispatching teams to commit the deed. Another plot involved furnishing weapons and other assassination devices to a Cuban dissident [rebel]. The proposed assassination devices ran the gamut from high-powered rifles to poison pills, poison pens, deadly bacterial powders, and other devices which strain the imagination. . . .

Efforts against Castro did not begin with assassination attempts.

From March through August 1960, during the last year of the Eisenhower Administration, the CIA considered plans to undermine Castro's charismatic appeal by sabotaging his speeches. According to the 1967 Report of the CIA's Inspector General, an official in the Technical Services Division (TSD) recalled discussing a scheme to spray Castro's broadcasting studio with a chemical which produced effects similar to LSD, but the scheme was rejected because the chemical was unreliable. During this period, TSD impregnated a box of cigars with a chemical which produced temporary disorientation, hoping to induce Castro to smoke one of the cigars before delivering a speech. The Inspector General also reported a plan to destroy Castro's image as "The Beard" by dusting his shoes with thallium salts, a strong depilatory [hair removal substance] that would cause his beard to fall out. The depilatory was to be administered during a trip outside Cuba, when it was anticipated Castro would leave his shoes outside the door of his hotel room to be shined. TSD procured the chemical and

tested it on animals, but apparently abandoned the scheme because Castro cancelled his trip. . . .

A notation in the records of the Operations Division, CIA's Office of Medical Services, indicates that on August 16, 1960, an official was given a box of Castro's favorite cigars with instructions to treat them with

Cuban leader Fidel Castro sparked the ire of American officials, some of whom devised plots to kill him.

lethal poison. The cigars were contaminated with a botulinum toxin so potent that a person would die after putting one in his mouth. The official reported that the cigars were ready on October 7, 1960; TSD notes indicate that they were delivered to an unidentified person on February 13, 1961. The record does not disclose whether an attempt was made to pass the cigars to Castro.

In August 1960, the CIA took steps to enlist members of the criminal underworld with gambling syndicate contacts to aid in assassinating Castro. . . . The earliest concrete evidence of the operation is a conversation between DDP [Deputy Director for Plans Richard] Bissell and Colonel Sheffield Edwards, Director of the Office of Security. Edwards recalled that Bissell asked him to locate someone who could assassinate Castro. Bissell confirmed that he requested Edwards to find someone to assassinate Castro and believed that Edwards raised the idea of contacting members of a gambling syndicate operating in Cuba. Edwards assigned the mission to the Chief of the Operational Support Division of the Office of Security. The Support Chief recalled that Edwards had said that he and Bissell were looking for someone to "eliminate" or "assassinate" Castro.

Edwards and the Support Chief decided to rely on Robert A. Maheu to recruit someone "tough enough" to handle the job. Maheu was an ex-FBI agent who had entered into a career as a private investigator in 1954. A former FBI associate of Maheu's was employed in the CIA's Office of Security and had arranged for the CIA to use Maheu in several sensitive covert operations in which "he didn't want to have an Agency person or a government person get caught.". . . Sometime in late August or early September 1960, the Support Chief approached Maheu about the proposed operation. As Maheu recalls the conversation, the Support Chief asked him to contact John Rosselli, an underworld figure with possible gambling contacts in Las Vegas, to determine if he would participate in a plan to "dispose" of Castro. . . . Maheu had known Rosselli since the late 1950's. Although Maheu claims not to have been aware of the extent of Rosselli's underworld connections and activities, he recalled that "it was certainly evident to me that he was able to accomplish things in Las Vegas when nobody else seemed to get the same kind of attention." . . .

According to Rosselli, he and Maheu met at the Brown Derby Restaurant in Beverly Hills in early September 1960. Rosselli testified that Maheu told him that "high government officials" needed his cooperation in getting rid of Castro, and that he asked him to help recruit Cubans to do the job. . . .

It was arranged that Rosselli would go to Florida and recruit Cubans for the operation. . . .

After Rosselli and Maheu had been in Miami for a short time . . . Rosselli introduced Maheu to two individuals on whom Rosselli intended to rely: "Sam Gold," who would serve as a "back-up man," or "key" man and "Joe," whom "Gold" said would serve as a courier to Cuba and make arrangements there. . . .

The Support Chief testified that he learned the true identities of his associates one morning when Maheu called and asked him to examine the "Parade" supplement to the *Miami Times* [newspaper]. An article on the Attorney General's ten-most-wanted criminals list revealed that "Sam Gold" was Momo Salvatore Giancana, a Chicago-based gangster, and "Joe" was Santos Trafficante, the Cosa Nostra chieftain in Cuba. . . . The Support Chief testified that this incident occurred after "we were up to our ears in it [the assassination plot]," a month or so after Giancana had been brought into the operation, but prior to giving the poison pills to Rosselli.

Maheu recalled that it was Giancana's job to locate someone in Castro's entourage who could accomplish the assassination, and that he met almost daily with Giancana over a substantial period of time. . . .

The Inspector General's Report described conversations among Bissell, Edwards, and the Chief of the Technical Services Division (TSD), concerning the most effective method of poisoning Castro. There is some evidence that Giancana or Rosselli originated the idea of depositing a poison pill in Castro's drink to give the "asset" [assassin] a chance to escape. The Support Chief recalled Rosselli's request for something "nice and clean, without getting into any kind of out and out ambushing," preferably a poison that would disappear

without a trace. The Inspector General's Report cited the Support Chief as stating that the Agency had first considered a "gangland-style killing" in which Castro would be gunned down. Giancana reportedly opposed the idea because it would be difficult to recruit someone for such a dangerous operation, and suggested instead the use of poison.

Edwards rejected the first batch of pills prepared by TSD because they would not dissolve in water. A second batch, containing botulinum toxin, "did the job expected of them" when tested on monkeys. The Support Chief received the pills from TSD, probably in February 1961, with assurances that they were lethal, and then gave them to Rosselli.

The record clearly establishes that the pills were given to a Cuban for delivery to the island some time prior to . . . mid-April 1961. . . . The Inspector General's Report states that in late February or March 1961, Rosselli reported to the Support Chief that the pills had been delivered to an official close to Castro who may have received kickbacks from the gambling interests. The Report states that the official returned the pills after a few weeks, perhaps because he had lost his position in the Cuban Government, and thus access to Castro, before he received the pills. The Report concludes that yet another attempt was made in April 1961, with the aid of a leading figure in the Cuban exile movement.

U.S. Senate, investigative committee report on CIA assassination plots against Castro, 1960–1965, 1975.

Johnson Explains Vietnam Policy

By February 1966, so many American were questioning U.S. actions in Vietnam that President Lyndon Johnson felt obliged to explain his policies. He did so after receiving the National Freedom Award in New York City. In the speech excerpted below, Johnson leaves little doubt that he intends for the United States to stand behind South Vietnam for as long as it takes to defeat Communist North Vietnam.

Tonight in Viet-Nam more than 200,000 of your young Americans stand there fighting for your freedom. Tonight our people are determined that these men shall have whatever help they need and that their cause, which is our cause, shall be sustained.

But in these last days there have been questions about what we are doing in Viet-Nam, and these questions have been answered loudly and clearly for every citizen to see and to hear. The strength of America can never be sapped by discussion, and we have no better nor stronger tradition than open debate, free debate, in hours of danger. We believe . . . that men are never so likely to settle a question rightly as when they discuss it freely. We are united in our commitment to free discussion. So also we are united in our determination that no foe anywhere should ever mistake our arguments for indecision, nor our debates for weakness.

So what are the questions that are still being asked?

First, some ask if this is a war for unlimited objectives. The answer is plain. The answer is "No."

Our purpose in Viet-Nam is to prevent the success of aggression. It is not conquest; it is not empire; it is not foreign bases; it is not domination. It is, simply put, just to prevent the forceful conquest of South Viet-Nam by North Viet-Nam.

Second, some people ask if we are caught in a blind escalation [expansion] of force that is pulling us headlong toward a wider war that no one wants. The answer, again, is a simple "No."

We are using that force and only that force that is necessary to stop this aggression. Our fighting men are in Viet-Nam because tens of thousands of invaders came south before them. Our numbers have increased in Viet-Nam because the aggression of others has increased in Viet-Nam. The high hopes of the aggressor have been dimmed and the tide of the battle has been turned, and our measured use of force will and must be continued. But this is prudent [practical] firmness under what I believe is careful control. There is not, and there will not be, a mindless escalation.

Third, others ask if our fighting men are to be denied the help they need. The answer, again, is and will be a resounding "No."

Our great military establishment has moved 200,000 men across 10,000 miles since last spring. These men have, and will have, all they need to fight the aggressor. They have already performed miracles in combat. The men behind them have worked miracles of supply, building new ports, transporting new equipment, opening new roads. The American forces of freedom are strong tonight in South Viet-Nam, and we plan to keep them so.

As you know, they are led there by a brilliant and a resourceful commander, General William C. Westmoreland. He knows the needs of war, and he supports the works of peace. And when he asks for more Americans to help the men that he has, his requests will be immediately studied and, as I promised the Nation last July, his needs will be immediately met.

Fourth, some ask if our men go alone to Viet-Nam, if we alone respect our great commitment in the Southeast Asia treaty. Still again, the answer is a simple "No." . . .

Fifth, some ask about the risks of a wider war, perhaps against the vast land armies of Red [Communist] China. And again the answer is "No," never by any act of ours—and not if there is any reason left behind the wild words from [the Chinese Capital] Peking.

American soldiers prepare to board a helicopter in Vietnam.

We have threatened no one, and we will not. We seek the end of no regime, and we will not. Our purpose is solely to defend against aggression. To any armed attack we will reply. We have measured the strength and the weakness of others, and we think we know our own. We observe in ourselves, and we applaud in others, a careful restraint in action. We can live with anger in word as long as it is matched by caution in deed.

The War on Want

Sixth, men ask if we rely on guns alone. Still again, the answer is "No.". . .

From the clear pledge which joins us with our allies, there has emerged a common dedication to the peaceful progress of the people of Viet-Nam—to schools for their children, to care for their health, to hope and bounty for their land.

The Vice President returned tonight from his constructive and very highly successful visit to [the South Vietnam capital of] Saigon and to other capitals, and he tells me that he and Ambassador [Henry Cabot] Lodge have found a new conviction and purpose in South Viet-Nam— for the battle against want and injustice as well as the battle against aggression. . . .

We Americans must understand how fundamental is the meaning of this second war—the war on want. I talked on my ranch last fall with Secretary [Orville] Freeman, the Secretary of Agriculture, and in my office last week with Secretary [John W.] Gardner, Secretary of Health, Education,

and Welfare, making, over and and over again, the same central point: The breeding ground of war is human misery. If we are not to fight forever in faraway places— in Europe, or the far Pacific, or the jungles of Africa, or the suburbs of Santo Domingo [Dominican Republic]—then we just must learn to get at the roots of violence. As a nation we must magnify our struggle against world hunger and illiteracy and disease. We must bring hope to men whose lives now end at two score [forty years] or less. Because without that hope, without progress in this war on want, we will be called on again to fight again and again, as we are fighting tonight.

Seventh, men ask who has a right to rule in South Viet-Nam. Our answer there is what it has been for 200 years. The people must have this right—the South Vietnamese people—and no one else.

Washington will not impose upon the people of South Viet-Nam a government not of their choice. Hanoi [capital of North Vietnam] shall not impose upon the people of South Viet-Nam a government not of their choice. So we will insist for ourselves on what we require from Hanoi: respect for the principle of government by the consent of the governed. We stand for self-determination—for free elections— and we will honor their result.

Eighth, men ask if we are neglecting any hopeful chance of peace. And the answer is "No."

A great servant of peace, Secretary Dean Rusk, has sent the message of peace on every wire and by every hand to every continent. A great pleader for peace here with us tonight, Ambassador Arthur Goldberg, has worked at home and abroad in this same cause. Their undiscouraged efforts will continue.

How much wiser it would have been, how much more compassionate toward its own people, if Hanoi had only come to the bargaining table at the close of the year. Then the 7,000 Communist troops who have died in battle since January the first, and the many thousands who have been wounded in that same period, would have lived in peace with their fellow men.

Today, as then, Hanoi has the opportunity to end the increasing toll the war is taking on those under its command.

Ninth, some ask how long we must bear this burden. To that question, in all honesty, I can give you no answer tonight. . . .

If the aggressor persists in Viet-Nam, the struggle may well be long. Our men in battle know and they accept this hard fact. We who are at home can do as much, because there is no computer that can tell the hour and the day of peace, but we do know that it will come only to the steadfast and never to the weak in heart.

Tenth, and finally, men ask if it is worth it. I think you know that answer. It is the answer that Americans have given for a quarter of a century, wherever American strength has been pledged to prevent aggression.

The contest in Viet-Nam is confused and hard, and many of its forms are new.

Yet our American purpose and policy are unchanged. Our men in Viet-Nam are there. They are there, as Secretary Dillon [former Secretary of the Treasury Douglas Dillon] told you, to keep a promise that was made 12 years ago. The Southeast Asia treaty promised, as Secretary John Foster Dulles said for the United States, that "an attack upon the treaty area would occasion [cause] a reaction so united, so strong, and so well placed that the aggressor would lose more than it could hope to gain."

Lyndon Johnson, address to Freedom House, New York City, February 23, 1966. Department of State Publication 8048. DC: U.S. Government Printing Office, 1966.

Students Question Vietnam Policies

In December 1966, after the United States had been fighting in Vietnam for more than a year, one hundred student leaders signed a letter, written by student Robert Powell, to President Lyndon Johnson questioning government policies in Vietnam. Powell and the other students were concerned that the goal the government said it hoped to achieve, peaceful negotiations to end the war, conflicted with the war's bloody, destructive reality. In the letter, printed in its entirety below, Powell expresses this concern and others about American involvement in Vietnam.

In your talk to the student interns last summer, as on other occasions, you have recognized and discussed problems that have been troubling members of our generation. We have been grateful for your

Students protest American involvement in Vietnam.

concern and encouraged by your invitation to express some of our thoughts.

Since many of these thoughts center increasingly on the situation in Vietnam, the New Year's renewal of the truce seems a suitable occasion to report to you that significant and growing numbers of our contemporaries [peers] are deeply troubled about the posture of their Government in Vietnam. We believe the state of mind of these people, though largely unreported, is of great importance, because

there are many who are deeply troubled for every one who has been outspoken in dissent [disagreement].

A great many of those faced with the prospect of military duty find it hard to square [reconcile] performance of that duty with concepts of personal integrity and conscience. Even more are torn by reluctance to participate in a war whose toll in property and life keeps escalating [growing], but about whose purpose and value to the United States they remain unclear.

The truces have highlighted a growing conviction on American campuses that if our objective in the fighting in Vietnam is a negotiated settlement rather than a military "victory," continued escalation cannot be justified by the failure of the other side to negotiate. If, on the other hand, our objective is no longer a negotiated settlement, the nature and attainability [ability to achieve] of our objectives in Vietnam raise serious new doubts. There is thus increasing confusion about both our basic purpose and our tactics, and there is increasing fear that the course now being pursued may lead us irrevocably [unavoidably] into a major land war in Asia—a war which many feel could not be won without recourse to nuclear weapons, if then.

In this context there is widespread support for the suggestion of the Pope and others that the resumed truce be extended . . . by restraint on both sides, even if no formal agreement is achieved. And there is hope that if fighting must be resumed in 1967 it will be resumed on a reduced scale.

In short, Mr. President, a great many of our contemporaries, raised in the democratic tradition of thinking for themselves, are finding a growing conflict between their own observations on the one hand, and statements by Administration [government] leaders about the war on the other. These are people as devoted to the Constitution, to the democratic process, and to law and order as were their fathers and brothers who served willingly in two World Wars and in Korea.

Unless this conflict can be eased, the United States will continue to find some of her most loyal and courageous young people choosing to go to jail rather than to bear their country's arms, while countless others condone or even utilize techniques for evading their legal obligations [of serving in the military]. Contributing to this situation is the almost universal conviction that the present Selective Service Law [that oversees the draft] operates unfairly.

Questions from Students

We write in the hope that this letter will encourage a frank discussion of these problems. If such a discussion clarified American objectives in Vietnam, it might help reverse the drift, which is now from confusion toward disaffection [disagreement]. To this end, we submit for your consideration some of the questions now agitating [disturbing] the academic community:

There is doubt that America's vital interests are sufficiently threatened in Vietnam to necessitate the growing commitment there.

There is doubt that such vital interests as may be threatened are best protected by this growing commitment.

There is doubt that a war which may devastate much of the countryside can lead to the stable and prosperous Vietnam we once hoped our presence would help create.

There is considerable concern about apparent contradictions in the American position on certain points basic to any efforts to negotiate a settlement. High Government officials reiterate [say repeatedly] our eagerness to negotiate "unconditionally," but we remain unclear about our willingness to accept full participation by the Viet Cong [Vietnamese Communists] as an independent party to negotiations. Similarly, Administration spokesmen reiterate our commitment to self-determination for South Vietnam [independence], but we remain unclear about our willingness to accept a coalition (or pro-Communist) government should the people of Vietnam eventually choose such a government under adequate international supervision.

Finally, Mr. President, we must report a growing sense—reinforced by [*New York Times* reporter] Harrison Salisbury's recent reports from Hanoi—that too often there is a wide disparity [contradiction] between American statements about Vietnam and American actions there.

We hope you will find it possible to share your thoughts with us about these matters. The rising confusion about national purposes can undermine mutual trust and respect among our people. This seems to us as urgent a problem as any that confronts the Nation today.

Robert Powell, letter of protest to President Johnson, December 29, 1966. Department of State Publication 8190. Washington, DC: U.S. Government Printing Office, 1967.

Lessons Learned in Vietnam

Millions of Americans objected to the war in Vietnam, blaming one of the conflict's chief ar- *chitects, Secretary of Defense Robert McNamara, for sinking the United States into a bloody and expensive quagmire. In 1995, McNamara revealed in his book* In Retrospect *that even he began to question the U.S. campaign in Vietnam as early as 1966, around the time he quit the Lyndon Johnson administration. McNamara remained silent about his concerns, however, even though the war dragged on for another seven years. In the following excerpt, the former secretary of defense attempts to explain why the U.S. mission failed in Vietnam.*

My involvement with Vietnam ended the day after I left the East Room [of the White House]. The war, of course, went on for another seven years. By the time [the] United States finally left South Vietnam in 1973 we had lost over 58,000 men and women; our economy had been damaged by years of heavy and improperly financed war spending; and the political unity of our society had been shattered, not to be restored for decades.

Were such high costs justified?

Dean Rusk, Walt Rostow, Lee Kwan Yew, and many other geopoliticians across the globe to this day answer yes. They conclude that without U.S. intervention in Vietnam, Communist hegemony [domination]— both Soviet and Chinese—would have spread farther through South and East Asia to include control of Indonesia, Thailand, and possibly India. Some would go further and say that the USSR would have been led to take greater risks to extend its influence elsewhere in the world, particularly in the Middle East, where it might well have sought control of the oil-producing nations. They might be correct, but I seriously question such judgments.

When the archives of the former Soviet Union, China, and Vietnam are opened to scholars, we will know more about those countries' intentions, but even without such knowledge we know that the danger of Communist aggression during the four decades of the Cold War was real and substantial. Although during the 1950s, 1960s, 1970s, and 1980s the West often misperceived, and therefore exaggerated, the power of the East and its ability to project that power, to have failed to defend ourselves against the threat would have been foolhardy and irresponsible.

That said, today I question whether either Soviet or Chinese behavior and influence in the 1970s and 1980s would have been materially different had the United States not entered the war in Indochina or had we withdrawn from Vietnam in the early or mid-1960s. By then it should have become apparent that the two conditions underlying President [John F.] Kennedy's decision to send military advisers to South Vietnam [in the early 1960s] were not being met and, indeed, could not be met: political stability did not exist and was unlikely ever to be achieved; and the South Vietnamese, even with our training assistance and logistical support, were incapable of defending themselves.

Given these facts—and they are facts—I believe we could and should have withdrawn from South Vietnam either in late

Robert McNamara, secretary of defense in the Johnson administration, points to strategic military sites on a map of Vietnam.

1963 amid the turmoil following [South Vietnamese president Ngo Dinh] Diem's assassination or in late 1964 or early 1965 in the face of increasing political and military weakness in South Vietnam. . . .

I do not believe that U.S. withdrawal at any of these junctures, if properly explained to the American people and to the world, would have led West Europeans to question . . . our guarantee of their security. Nor do I believe that Japan would have viewed our security treaties as any less credible. On the contrary, it is possible we would have improved our credibility by withdrawing from Vietnam and saving our strength for more defensible stands elsewhere. . . .

It is sometimes said that the post–Cold War world will be so different from the world of the past that the lessons of Vietnam will be . . . of no relevance to the twenty-first century. I disagree. That said, if we are to learn from our experience in Vietnam, we must first pinpoint our failures. There were eleven major causes for our disaster in Vietnam:

1. We misjudged then—as we have since—the . . . intentions of our adversaries (in this case, North Vietnam and the Vietcong, supported by China and the Soviet Union), and we exaggerated the dangers to the United States of their actions.

2. We viewed the people and leaders of South Vietnam in terms of our own experience. We saw in them a thirst for—and a determination to fight for—freedom and democracy. We totally misjudged the political forces within the country.

3. We underestimated the power of nationalism to motivate a people (in this case, the North Vietnamese and Vietcong) to fight and die for their beliefs and values—and we continue to do so today in many parts of the world.

4. Our misjudgments of friend and foe alike reflected our profound ignorance of the history, culture, and politics of the people in the area, and the personalities and habits of their leaders. . . .

5. We failed then—as we have since—to recognize the limitations of modern, high-technology military equipment, forces, and doctrine in confronting unconventional, highly motivated people's movements. We failed as well to adapt our military tactics to the task of winning the hearts and minds of people from a totally different culture.

Years after the Vietnam War, Robert McNamara speaks to the North Vietnamese press about American actions in Vietnam.

6. We failed to draw Congress and the American people into a full and frank discussion and debate of the pros and cons of a large-scale U.S. military involvement in Southeast Asia before we initiated the action.

7. After the action got under way and unanticipated events forced us off our planned course, we failed to retain popular support in part because we did not explain fully what was happening and why we were doing what we did. We had not prepared the public to understand the complex events we faced and how to react constructively to the need for changes in course as the nation confronted uncharted seas and an alien environment. A nation's deepest strength lies not in its military prowess but, rather, in the unity of its people. We failed to maintain it.

8. We did not recognize that neither our people nor our leaders are omniscient [all-knowing]. Where our own security is not directly at stake, our judgment of what is in another people's or country's best interest should be put to the test of open discussion in international forums. We do not have the God-given right to shape every nation in our own image or as we choose.

9. We did not hold to the principle that U.S. military action—other than in response to direct threats to our own security—should be carried out only in conjunction with multinational forces supported fully (and not merely cosmetically) by the international community.

10. We failed to recognize that in international affairs, as in other aspects of life, there may be problems for which there are no immediate solutions. For one whose life has been dedicated to the belief and practice of problem solving, this is particularly hard to admit. But, at times, we may have to live with an imperfect, untidy world.

11. Underlying many of these errors lay our failure to organize the top echelons [layers] of the executive branch to deal effectively with the extraordinarily complex range of political and military issues, involving the great risks and costs—including, above all else, loss of life—associated with the application of military force under substantial constraints over a long period of time. Such organizational weakness would have been costly had this been the only task confronting the president and his advisers. It, of course, was not. It coexisted with the wide array of other domestic and international problems confronting us. We thus failed to analyze and debate our actions in Southeast Asia—our objectives, the risks and costs of alternative ways of dealing with them, and the necessity of changing course when failure was clear—with the intensity and thoroughness that characterized the debates of the Executive Committee during the Cuban Missile Crisis.

These were our major failures, in their essence. Though set forth separately, they are all in some way linked: failure in one area contributed to or compounded failure in another. Each became a turn in a terrible knot.

★ Chapter 5 ★

The End of the Cold War

or more than forty years, the unsettling deadlock between the two superpowers dominated headlines around the world. Many people believed that the Cold War might last well into the twenty-first century, if not forever. Thus, when the Soviet Union began to collapse in the late 1980s, few observers were prepared for the dizzying speed at which the Cold War ground to a halt.

By the mid-1980s, it was obvious to many people in the Soviet Union that their economic system was in ruins. Their standard of living was dropping dramatically, and citizens faced shortages of basic consumer goods such as food, clothing, and appliances. And because of the shortages, Soviet people were forced to spend one-third of their waking hours waiting in lines at shops that sold basic items such as bread, potatoes, and meat. When Mikhail Gorbachev, a charismatic personality and one of the youngest men to run the U.S.S.R. was named premier in 1985, he

pledged to do something about these problems.

Gorbachev set out on a program of reshaping the Soviet Union to fit into the modern world. He purged the government of hundreds of senior officials who were in their eighties and nineties and shocked Soviet citizens by becoming the first premier to appear in public to shake hands and listen to their problems. Gorbachev also appeared on television and empathized with the average person's complaints about food shortages, poor health care, and shoddy consumer products. No other Soviet leader had mentioned such failings of communism.

In an effort to change things, Gorbachev announced his plan to rebuild the nation. It was called perestroika—a Russian word meaning "economic reconstruction." Perestroika, in turn, ushered in glasnost, a period of Soviet history in which the government pledged less talk and more honesty, openness, and action. Ultimately, perestroika could not stop the downward spiral of the Soviet economy, but glasnost did help change the country by inspiring average citizens to question government policy.

Gorbachev also realized that the U.S.S.R. could no longer afford to maintain a huge military presence in Eastern bloc countries, so the premier insisted that each nation become independent, something most countries had wanted for years. No longer would Soviet tanks and soldiers swarm into these nations to crush dissent as they had in earlier decades.

Soviet leader Mikhail Gorbachev presided over economic reconstruction efforts after dismantling his nation's communist system.

By 1989, Poland, Hungary, and Czechoslovakia had formed independent governments. Then, on November 8 of that year, East Germany's leader, Egon Krenz, decided to allow East Germans, who for decades had been denied the freedom to leave Communist East Berlin, to emigrate to democratic West Berlin. When he opened the gate in the Berlin Wall, a physical barrier that had stood for decades as a symbol of the division between democracy and communism, East Germans flooded into the West. With the gate's armed guards removed, thousands of citizens on both sides began to hammer away at the wall. The next day, November 9, 1989, the wall came tumbling down.

The Soviet Union was also crumbling. In 1990, bankrupt and humiliated, the Communist Party relinquished control in the Soviet Union after nearly seventy years, and the country ceased to exist. The U.S.S.R. was divided into several independent countries called the Commonwealth of Independent States. The bitter military and ideological enemy of the United States had collapsed, and the Cold War was over.

Mikhail Gorbachev Explains Perestroika

By the mid-1980s, it was obvious to Soviet leaders that the U.S.S.R. was falling behind the rest of the world in almost every economic and social sector. When Mikhail Gorbachev became premier of the U.S.S.R. in 1985, he announced a re-building program called perestroika. This historic event marked the first time in nearly seventy years of Soviet history that the government had admitted there were large-scale problems. In the following excerpt, Gorbachev explains the reasons he believed perestroika was necessary.

What is perestroika? What prompted the idea of restructuring? What does it mean in the history of socialism? What does it augur for the peoples of the Soviet Union? How might it influence the outside world? All these questions concern the world public and are being actively discussed. Let me begin with the first one.

Perestroika—An Urgent Necessity

I think one thing should be borne in mind when studying the origins and essence of perestroika in the USSR. Perestroika is no whim on the part of some ambitious individuals or a group of leaders. If it were, no exhortations [urgent appeals], plenary meetings or even a party congress could have rallied the people to the work which we are now doing and which involves more and more Soviet people each day.

Perestroika is an urgent necessity arising from the profound processes of development in our socialist society. This society is ripe for change. It has long been yearning for it. Any delay in beginning perestroika could have led to . . . serious social, economic and political crises.

We have drawn these conclusions from a broad and frank analysis of the situation that has developed in our society by the middle of the eighties. This situation and the problems arising from it presently confront the country's leadership, in which new people have gradually appeared in the last few years. I would like to discuss here the main results of this analysis. . . .

Let me first explain the far-from-simple situation which had developed in the country by the eighties and which made perestroika necessary and inevitable.

At some stage—this became particularly clear in the latter half of the seventies—something happened that was at first sight inexplicable. The country began to lose momentum. Economic failures became more frequent. Difficulties began to accumulate and deteriorate, and unresolved problems to multiply. Elements of what we call stagnation and other phenomena alien to socialism began to appear in the life of society. A kind of "braking mechanism" affecting social and economic development formed. And all this happened at a time when scientific and technological revolution opened up new prospects for economic and social progress. . . .

A Country Losing Momentum

Analyzing the situation, we first discovered a slowing economic growth. In the last fifteen years the national income growth rates had declined by more than a half and by the beginning of the eighties had fallen to a level close to economic stagnation. A country that was once quickly closing on the world's advanced nations began to lose

Soviet industrial plants keep busy during difficult economic times.

one position after another. Moreover, the gap in the efficiency of production, quality of products, scientific and technological development, the production of advanced technology and the use of advanced techniques began to widen, and not to our advantage. . . .

There were costly projects that never lived up to the highest scientific and technological standards. The worker or the enterprise that had expended the greatest amount of labor, material and money was considered the best. It is natural for the producer to "please" the consumer, if I may put it that way. With us, however, the consumer found himself totally at the mercy of the producer and had to make do with what the latter chose to give him. . . .

It became typical of many of our economic executives to think not of how to build up the national asset, but of how to put more material, labor and working time into an item to sell it at a higher price. Consequently, for all "gross output," there was a shortage of goods. We spent, in fact we are still spending, far more on raw materials, energy and other resources per unit of output than other developed nations. Our country's wealth in terms of natural and manpower resources has spoilt, one may even say corrupted, us. . . .

An absurd situation was developing. The Soviet Union, the world's biggest producer of steel, raw materials, fuel and energy, has shortfalls in them due to wasteful or inefficient use. One of the biggest producers of grain for food, it nevertheless has to buy millions of tons of grain a year for fodder. We have the largest number of doctors and hospital beds per thousand of the population and, at the same time, there are glaring shortcomings in our health services. Our rockets can find Halley's comet and fly to Venus with amazing accuracy, but side by side with these scientific and technological triumphs is an obvious lack of efficiency in using scientific achievements for economic needs, and many Soviet household appliances are of poor quality. . . .

Not that that period should be painted solely in dark colors. The overwhelming majority of Soviet people worked honestly. Science, the economy and culture continued to develop. All the more inadmissible and painful, then, were the negative phenomena.

I think I have said enough for you to realize how serious the situation was and how urgent a thorough change was. The [Communist] Party has found the strength and the courage to soberly appraise [study] the situation and recognize that fundamental changes and transformations are indispensable.

An unbiased and honest approach led us to the only logical conclusion that the country was verging on crisis. This conclusion was announced at the April 1985 Plenary Meeting of the Central Committee [Soviet Congress], which inaugurated [began] the new strategy of perestroika and formulated its basic principles. . . .

By saying all this I want to make the reader understand that the energy for revolutionary change has been accumulating amid our people and in the Party for some time. And the ideas of perestroika have been prompted not just by pragmatic [practical] interests and considerations but also by our troubled conscience, by the indomitable [strong] commitment to ideals which we inherited from the Revolution and as a result of a theoretical quest which gave us a better knowledge of society and reinforced our determination to go ahead.

Mikhail Gorbachev, *Perestroika: New Thinking for Our Country and the World.* New York: Harper and Row, 1987.

Mikhail Gorbachev argued that perestroika reflected ideals voiced by Lenin (pictured) and other leaders of the revolution.

Historic Opportunities and Ominous Dangers

As the Soviet Union disintegrated, the United States joined the rest of the world in extending official diplomatic recognition to the newly independent former republics. In this December 1991 speech, Secretary of State James A. Baker expresses hope for the future but also voices concern about control over the former superpower's vast arsenal of nuclear weapons.

Whatever the original intentions of perestroika and glasnost, by early August of this year, the all-powerful Stalinist state was well on its way to dissolution. A new civil society was breaking out across the Soviet Union. Democracy was replacing communism; power was moving from the center to the republics; and the old centrally-planned economy was in the throes of collapse. . . .

The dramatic collapse of communism in Moscow and the unraveling of the centralized Soviet state confront the West with great opportunities as well as ominous dangers. Popularly-elected leaders now run large and strategically-important republics, including Russia, Ukraine, and Kazakhstan. They look to America and the West for guidance and help in launching genuine, far-reaching political and economic reform. If they can succeed, the centuries-old menace posed to the West, first by czarist autocracy and then by Soviet totalitarianism, will have been permanently altered.

The opportunities are historic:

• We have the chance to anchor Russia, Ukraine, and other republics firmly in the Euro-Atlantic community and democratic commonwealth of nations.

• We have the chance to bring democracy to lands that have little knowledge of it, an achievement that can transcend centuries of history.

• We have the chance to help harness the rich human and material resources of those vast lands to the cause of freedom instead of totalitarianism, thereby immeasurably enhancing the security, prosperity, and freedom of America and the world.

Yet the dangers are equal in scale to the opportunities:

• *Economically,* the old Soviet system has collapsed, multiplying every day the threats these reformers face—from social dislocation to political fragmentation to ethnic violence. Reconstructing economies that have been devastated by central planning is even more difficult than reconstructing from the devastation of war.

• *Politically,* the dangers of protracted anarchy and chaos are obvious. Great empires rarely go quietly into extinction. No one can dismiss the possibility that darker political forces lurk in the wings, representing the remnants of Stalinism or the birth of nationalist extremism or even fascism, ready to exploit the frustrations of a proud but exhausted people in their hour of despair.

• *Strategically,* both of these alternatives—anarchy or reaction—could become threats to the West's vital interests when they shake a land that is still home to nearly 30,000 nuclear weapons and the most powerful

A protester in Red Square holds a banner denouncing the Soviet government.

place—marks the challenge history has dealt us: to see the end of the Soviet Empire turned into a beginning for democracy and economic freedom in Russia and Ukraine, in Kazakhstan and Belarus, in Armenia, Kyrgyzstan, and elsewhere across the former Soviet Empire.

James A. Baker, "America and the Collapse of the Soviet Empire: What Has to Be Done," Vital Speeches of the Day, January 1, 1992.

Bush Declares a New World Order

In 1989, the Communists eased their totalitarian policies in the Soviet Union while relinquishing control in Poland, Hungary, and other Eastern European countries. On September 25, 1989, President George Bush addressed the opening session of the UN General Assembly and called the changes part of a "new world order." In the following excerpt from that speech, Bush speaks of a new era where repression and fear are replaced by freedom and democratic economic policies. Bush also calls on the UN to cooperate with the United States to solve environmental problems and eliminate threats from chemical and nuclear weapons.

arsenal of conventional weaponry ever amassed in Europe.

Taken together, these dangers serve as a call to action for America and the West. This historic watershed—the collapse of communist power in Bolshevism's birth-

The United Nations can play a fundamental role in the central issue of our time. For today, there's an idea at work around the globe—an idea of undeniable force; that idea is freedom.

Freedom's advance is evident everywhere. In central Europe, in Hungary—where state and society are now in the midst

of a movement toward political pluralism [coexistence] and a free market economy, where the barrier that once enforced an unnatural division between Hungary and its neighbors to the West has been torn down—torn down—replaced by a new hope for the future, a new hope in freedom.

We see freedom at work in Poland—where, in deference [respect] to the will of the people, the Communist Party has relinquished its monopoly on power and, indeed, in the Soviet Union—where the world hears the voices of people no longer afraid to speak out or to assert the right to rule themselves.

But freedom's march is not confined to a single continent or to the developed world alone. We see the rise of freedom in Latin America, where, one by one, dictatorships are giving way to democracy. We see it on the Continent of Africa—where more and more nations see, in the system of free enterprise, salvation for economies crippled by excessive state control. East and West, North and South, on every continent, we can see the outlines of a new world of freedom.

Of course, freedom's work remains unfinished. The trend we see is not yet universal. Some regimes still stand against the tide. Some rulers still deny the right of the people to govern themselves. But now, the power of prejudice and despotism [dictatorship] is challenged. Never before have these regimes stood so isolated and alone—so out of step with the steady advance of freedom.

Today we are witnessing . . . the demise of the totalitarian idea of the omniscient [all-knowing], all powerful state. There are many reasons for this collapse. But in the end, one fact alone explains what we see today: Advocates of the totalitarian idea saw its triumph written in the laws of

At the United Nations President George Bush gestures as he speaks about a new world order.

history. They failed to see the love of freedom that was written in the human heart.

Two hundred years ago today, the United States—our Congress—proposed the Bill of Rights—fundamental freedoms belonging to every individual; rights no government can deny. . . .

Make no mistake: Nothing can stand in the way of freedom's march. There will come a day when freedom is seen the world over to be a universal birthright—of every man and woman, of every race and walk of life. Even under the worst circumstances, at the darkest of times, freedom has always remained alive—a distant dream, perhaps, but always alive.

Today, that dream is no longer distant. For the first time—for millions around the world—a new world of freedom is within reach. Today is freedom's moment.

You see, the possibility now exists for the creation of a true community of nations—built on shared interests and ideals. A true community—a world where free governments and free markets meet the rising desire of the people to control their own destiny, to live in dignity, and to exercise freely their fundamental [basic] human rights. It is time we worked together to deliver that destiny into the hands of men and women everywhere.

Our challenge is to strengthen the foundations of freedom, encourage its advance, and face our most urgent challenges—the global challenges of the 21st century—economic health, environmental well-being, and the great questions of war and peace.

First, global economic growth. During this decade, a number of developing nations have moved into the ranks of the world's most advanced economies—all of them, each and every one, powered by the engine of free enterprise. . . . I believe we'll learn in the century ahead that many nations of the world have barely begun to tap their true potential for development. The free market and its fruits are not the special preserve of a few. They are a harvest that everyone can share.

Beyond the challenge of global growth lies another issue of global magnitude—the environment. No line drawn on a map can stop the advance of pollution. Threats to our environment have become international problems. We must develop an international approach to urgent environmental issues—one that seeks common solutions to common problems.

The United Nations is already at work—on the question of global warming, in the effort to prevent oil spills and other disasters from fouling our seas and the air we breathe.

And I will tell you now, the United States will do its part. We have committed ourselves to the worldwide phaseout of all chlorofluorocarbons [pollutants that destroy the ozone] by the year 2000. We've proposed amending our own Clean Air Act to ensure clean air for our citizens within a single generation. We've banned the import of ivory to protect the elephant and rhinoceros from the human predators who exterminate them for profit. . . . The environment belongs to all of us. In this new world of freedom, the world's citizens must enjoy this common trust for generations to come.

Global economic growth and the stewardship of our planet both are critical issues. But as always, questions of war and peace must be paramount [of great importance] to the United Nations.

We must move forward to limit—and eliminate—weapons of mass destruction. Five years ago, at the UN Conference on Disarmament in Geneva, I presented a U.S. draft treaty outlawing chemical weapons. Since then progress has been made, but time is running out. The threat is growing. More than 20 nations now possess chemical weapons or the capability to produce them. These horrible weapons are now finding their way into regional conflicts. This is simply unacceptable.

For the sake of mankind, we must halt and reverse this threat. Today I want to an-nounce steps that the United States is ready to take—steps to rid the world of these truly terrible weapons—toward a treaty that will ban—eliminate—all chemical weapons from the Earth 10 years from the day it is signed. . . .

We are serious about achieving conventional arms reductions as well. And that's why we tabled new proposals just last Thursday at the conventional [armed] forces in Europe negotiations in Vienna—proposals that demonstrate our commitment to act rapidly to ease military tensions in Europe and move the nations of that continent one step closer to their common destiny—a Europe whole and free. . . .

Each of these achievements is important in its own right, . . . but they are more important still as signs of a new attitude that prevails between the United States and the U.S.S.R. Serious differences remain—we know that—but the willingness to deal constructively and candidly with those differences is news that we and, indeed, the world must welcome.

George H.W. Bush, address to the United Nations, New York City, September 25, 1989.

★ Chronology of Events ★

1945

The United States drops atomic bombs on Hiroshima and Nagasaki in Japan.

1946

Winston Churchill delivers the "Iron Curtain" speech.

1947

The National Security Act creates the National Security Council (NSC) and the Central Intelligence Agency (CIA).

1949

The Soviets successfully test an atomic bomb; Communists take over China.

1950

Senator Joseph McCarthy says spies are in the State Department; Paul Nitze's NSC-68 promotes massive military buildup; North Korean invasion starts the Korean War.

1953

An armistice ends the fighting in Korea.

1954

Secretary of State John Foster Dulles propounds massive-retaliation policy; the U.S. Senate reins in Senator Joseph McCarthy; the French fall at Dien Bien Phu, Vietnam.

1957

The Soviets test an intercontinental missile; the Soviets launch *Sputnik I*, the first satellite.

1959

Fidel Castro takes power in Cuba; the United States showcases consumer goods in Moscow.

1961

Dwight Eisenhower warns of military-industrial power; the Soviets rapidly erect the Berlin Wall.

1962

The Cuban missile crisis approaches nuclear war.

1964

The United States and North Vietnam clash in the Gulf of Tonkin in Vietnam.

1968

North Vietnam pounds American positions during the Tet offensive; the Soviets invade Czechoslovakia.

1970

Richard Nixon expands the Vietnam War, invading Cambodia; four students are killed at Kent State University protesting the Vietnam War.

1972

The United States has an arms-control breakthrough with the Soviet Union.

1973

The Treaty of Paris means peace for the United States.

1974

Richard Nixon resigns as U.S. president.

1983

Ronald Reagan announces the Strategic Defense Initiative.

1985

Reformer Mikhail Gorbachev gets Soviet reins of power.

1987

Ronald Reagan and Mikhail Gorbachev sign an historic arms accord.

1989

The Berlin Wall comes down.

1990

East and West Germany reunify.

1991

The Union of Soviet Socialist Republics splits up.

☆ Index ☆

★ Picture Credits ★

★ About the Editor ★

Stuart A. Kallen is the author of more than 150 nonfiction books for children and young adults. He has written on topics ranging from the theory of relativity to rock-and-roll history, to life on the American frontier. In addition, Mr. Kallen has written award-winning children's videos and television scripts. In his spare time, Mr. Kallen is a singer/songwriter/guitarist in San Diego, California.